Life in the Foster Lane

Practical Insights on Fostering Teens

Lesia Knudsen

This book should be required reading for all new foster parents or anyone considering becoming a resource family. Lesia's advice on setting and encouraging positive and realistic expectations is a keystone in building strong, mutually beneficial relationships. Through her sincere sharing of successes and failures, Lesia offers a model for creating clear and safe boundaries for everyone, and unconditionally welcoming and loving all children. Whether you need optimism for sending a child on without you, courage to create a permanent plan, or healing from a challenging placement, this is a worthwhile read.

Annette Venables
President, Marin Foster Care
Association California

Lesia Knudsen tells it like it is about being a foster parent! If you want a book that is akin to a sit-down conversation with an experienced, real, and practical foster Mom, you've found it! This is a humorous, honest, encouraging, humble offering for any parent. This book is power-packed with wisdom, real life examples, and concrete plans. It is the good, the bad and the funny of foster parenting! Regardless of your station in life you want to read it!

Angele Navares
Foster Parent Recruiter,
Koinonia Foster Homes Nevada

This book should be an aid in foster training 101 and for all foster parents! Each child that comes to us comes with their own unique baggage, bumps, and bruises and we are there to mend the broken pieces the best we can. I hope each person that reads this booklet takes away some piece of knowledge with them.

Marlene Urbani
Foster Parent, Mississippi

Acknowledgements

I would like to say thank you to the loving, generous, and kind individuals who choose to foster—those who bravely take on the challenges of parenting children for parents who either can't or won't. Thank you to those of you who are considering becoming foster parents for being willing to freely give your love to children who are probably going through the hardest times of their lives.

Thank you to my fellow *life changers* who told their stories, imparting wisdom from their journeys of foster care into this book. You have shared your hearts and strength; this book is much better for it. May you be blessed for your sacrificial love and patience. It will never be forgotten, not by me or the children you've loved. Thank you, thank you, thank you.

"Children may not remember what we say but they always remember how we made them feel." (Anon.)

TABLE OF CONTENTS

INTRODUCTION

Being a foster parent can be rewarding, exciting, and satisfying. It can also be messy, confusing, and exhausting. It will cause you to grow and rethink many ideas and beliefs that you've held dear for a long time. Fostering often causes me to say to myself, "What the heck am I doing?" Then I remember. I'm giving the next generation a chance at life, and so are you. I am writing this book because I want to share with others what I wish someone had shared with me.

I love teens, know teens, and will admit that I'm gifted in my work with teens. I have been called the "Crazy Teen Lady," the "Teen Whisperer," and just plain "Crazy"! I'll accept all these titles proudly. I've worked with teens and their parents for over twenty years. My favorite teen is the one no one wants to deal with. That's why I choose to foster teens and to work with kids in the juvenile probation system. The purpose of this book is to give you some framework in working with teens in foster care, and to look at what mindset one needs in the fostering journey. Teens are a special breed and need the "right kind of crazy" to deal with them. I hope that after reading this you will say either, "I think I can do this," or, "Whew! I'm glad I read this before I said yes!" The goal is to make teen placements successful. If I can help you be *kinda, sorta, somewhat* mentally prepared, then that's half the battle. The other half happens in your home with your amazing teen!

I want to be as honest as possible. I don't list everything that you need to know because I don't know everything. I write things that I think are helpful from my own experience in fostering teens. I am sharing the basics that would have helped me keep my sanity if someone had just given me a heads up. Hopefully this will serve as your heads up, and save your sanity as you find ways to make this foster gig a little easier.

I'm not going to paint a nice, pretty picture of you and your foster teen sitting on the porch of a house with a white picket fence, sipping lemonade, holding hands, and singing Kumbaya. A real picture, sorry to say, has part of that white picket fence kicked down because you or your foster teen got angry! And if you can handle that picture…you can do anything! I could write about all the wonderful experiences so many foster parents have had and make you feel all warm and fuzzy inside and ready to *save the children*. You might feel good after reading it but it won't help you when things get a little rough. I want you to experience the *real deal*. The real deal may include kicked-in fences, but it also includes good times, loving times, and a real sense of family. I have included stories and experiences from other foster parents to bring you additional insight. There is a lot of wisdom out there.

One thing I know about fostering is this: foster kids need us! We have a world of lost, hurt, and abused kids who don't know up from down or right from wrong. They have never experienced real love and concern and are at a loss to conceive of who they are or who they were created to be. If one family will take the challenge and walk with that child through what may be his or her toughest times, a life could be changed. Fostering reminds me of the story of the little boy walking on the beach where hundreds of starfish are washed up on the shore. The little boy begins picking them up one at a time and throwing them back into the water. Someone walks by and says, "Why are you wasting your time? There are hundreds of starfish! You'll never save them all, so what does it matter?" The little boy replies, "It matters to this one." Maybe we can't save them all—we may not even be able to "save" the one we get in our home—but at least that one young person understands that someone cared, that someone listened, and someone loved. All we can do is try, and the rest is up to them.

The fostering journey is totally doable and you don't have to do it alone. Alrighty then, are you ready? Let's get this party started!!

A MOMENT IN THEIR SHOES

Imagine that one day you walk into work as usual and some strange person tells you that you no longer work there and that you must leave the building immediately. This person, whom you do not know, gives you no explanation. You are no longer employed. You may have to get on food stamps, and you may no longer be able to pay your rent or mortgage. Think about all the questions, concerns, and worries that you would have. Think about the stigma of being on public assistance or having to file bankruptcy, or even becoming homeless.

Again, imagine: Someone tells you that you can't live in your home anymore. There is mold. The inspector says that your house is toxic and you must leave—now! He doesn't know when you can move back in because of the health hazard. In fact, he tells you that everything you own is contaminated and you may NEVER be able to go back home! You leave with nothing except the clothes on your back. You long for your home even though it's toxic and dangerous—it's your home, the place you've always known and loved.

Now, let those scenarios sink in. What are you thinking? What are you feeling? The emotions, concerns, and questions swirling in your head as an adult are the same emotions, concerns, and questions that swirl around in the head of a foster child or teen. The difference is that foster children are still growing physically and emotionally and don't have the maturity to process such life-changing events. Can you imagine a young child or teen being taken away from everything they've known and loved, no matter how toxic? What about the stigma of being a "foster kid" and the shame that goes with that? As quiet as the Child and Family Services tries to keep it, it doesn't work. Once someone who is not the child's parent picks the child up from school, or they give a new address to the school administration, the secret is out and the embarrassment and humiliation come flooding in!

Foster kids have so many questions and so few answers—questions like, why am I leaving my parents? Did I do something wrong? Whose fault is it? What did my parents do? When am I going home? Why can't I go with people who look like me? How am I going to get my hair done? I don't want to leave my friends; will I see them again? What about my brother and sister? What does this person know about me? Will they judge me? The list goes on and on. They aren't playing twenty questions—these are very real issues they need answered in order to make sense of what's happening. They are trying to figure out how to survive the unknown and wrap their head around what is probably the most confusing and devastating time in their lives!

Why did I ask you to engage in this exercise? Because there's so much more to fostering than just opening your amazing home and loving a child in need. It goes beyond a safe place, food, and clothing. It also requires spending a moment in their shoes. I believe if we stand in their Van's, Chanclas (Mexican flip-flop), or Nikes, it will change the way we view the foster child. Maybe it will help explain why they do some of the things they do and say the things they say. The anger, the acting out, being clingy, and a hundred other unexpected attitudes and behaviors may show up immediately or within a few weeks of their entry into your home. You may get the child who is so happy to be with you, and things are amazing from day one. They like you, you like them, and life is beautiful!

Most of the time there is a honeymoon phase where everything is "golden." Your foster kid is polite and is everything you've wanted and imagined in a foster child. Eventually the honeymoon ends, and the "*I'm trying to make sense of this whole crazy experience the best way I know how, and this is what it looks like*" kid comes out.

Taking the time to understand them and their situation may help you realize that it's not personal. It's not personal when they treat you like you're the enemy instead of the one who "rescued" them. And when they do or say things that make no sense, you can stop and remember that it's really not you, it's them being overwhelmed and scared, missing family, and not equipped to process all that is happening to them. Please know that these aren't bad kids. These are kids caught up in a bad situation.

I'm not encouraging sympathy—I'm advocating for empathy. I'm not saying to let them get away with anything and everything because they caught a tough break. I DO NOT want you to pity them. Being pitied and patronized is the last thing that a child, especially a teen, wants from you. What they do want is respect, understanding, and a chance.

I pray that you will come to marvel at the strength and courage of the ones that will enter into your home. I pray you are encouraged to cheer on these young people as you watch them do the best they can with the terrible hand they've been dealt. Foster kids are survivors! It's our job to love them and provide them with a safe place to rest, detox, and breathe. We have the privilege of helping them make the best "plays" with the lousy cards they have in their hand, as much as they will let us.

This is an amazing journey and we have to be just as courageous as these beautiful children. We need to be determined enough to endure the inconvenience of a misbehaving child. We have to be empathetic enough to understand that these kids may know nothing about life, family, house rules, or basic life skills, and walk with them through a huge learning process with love, grace, structure, and kindness.

I know this may make some of you a little nervous, but guess what? We are well equipped to do this thing called fostering and to do it well! We don't have to be perfect—we just have to give it our best. And as we'll discuss later, you are not doing it alone.

Be strong my friends, you got this!

"Be strong and courageous. Do not be afraid; do not be discouraged, for the Lord your God will be with you wherever you go" (Joshua 1:9 NIV)

WHY?

I remember when my kids were toddlers and the question *Why?* seemed to come at me hundreds of times in the course of a day. Now I realize that question is key in everything we choose to do in life. Our *why* is what motivates us. This applies to becoming foster parents. Some of the questions my family has had to come face to face with are, "Why are we doing this?" "What are we as a family expecting to gain?" "What are we expecting from the foster kids by bringing them into this family?"

These core questions serve as an invitation to look deeply and honestly at our motivations. Let's look at some possible reasons you might be considering the fostering journey:

- Because I love teens

- Because we have a lot to give

- Because my family is so awesome

- Because we can't have children

- There is an extra room in the house, so why not?

- Because I have a lot of love

- Because I want to feel needed

- Because we need some extra money

- Because I want to help kids in need

The list of possible reasons could go on and on. All of them are valid reasons. Whatever your *why* is, make sure it's pure—that there are no hidden agendas or unspoken underlying motives.

The *why* leads to the next important question: "*What am I expecting?*" That may seem like an odd question because we as foster families usually do what we do in order to *give,* not to *get.* But there is always a payoff, something we get in return for what we give. The payoff might be the satisfaction of helping this generation, or it could be the filling of a personal void. Perhaps fostering makes you feel needed. Or maybe the payoff is the joy of knowing that you gave a child love and a safe place. The payoff needs to be examined, and here's why: if we aren't aware of our real needs or motives in bringing these beautiful kids into our home, we could be seriously disappointed or disillusioned.

For example, if our sole reason for providing foster care is because it is our passion to prepare them for the future and impart wisdom, and then they reject us or flunk out of school, where does that leave us? It would be easy in that case to feel like a failure, frustrated or angry because our words of wisdom were not heeded. The fact is that when we foster for any other reason than the foster kids themselves and their needs, disappointment is inevitable. The goal of all we do should be *them*—what *they* need, what *they* want. I'm not saying that we as foster parents shouldn't want appreciation or love, but we can't build what we do on our needs and unsatisfied hungers. The foster child has to be the focus, not us. I'm also not saying that the foster child should be entitled to everything they say or think they need, because of course limit-setting is very much part of the landscape of any family.

Let me give you an example: I work with kids in the juvenile probation system, offering them life-coaching, mentoring, and whatever else they needed. My passion, desire, and call in life is to equip young people to be successful, confident, and an asset to society. I ran a program in Reno/ Sparks, Nevada called *I Have Hope and A Future Mentoring Program*. I mentored about fifteen girls who were "at risk" and attended one of the "worst" schools in the area. Eleven graduated high school and either went on to college, trade school, the military, or are working. SUCCESS! I keep in touch with most of them to this day.

Sometime later I came to California and started working with the great kids in the juvenile system. I had a great relationship with them and they loved me, however NONE of them was a "success" for me, including the young lady that I mentored then fostered. I wanted to see these kids thrive, get jobs, go to school, and reach their goals. Instead they made repeated trips to juvenile hall, were sent away to placement, or flunked school and smoked weed.

My foster daughter was not passing high school, did not have a job and was not confident in who she was. She was, instead, tied up in personal drama, emotional upheaval, and depression. My confidence and faith in what I felt I was called to do was ROCKED. I wanted to quit, fell into depression, and just wanted to walk away. Then I asked myself, "Why am I doing this? Is it to impart the skills they need to be successful? Or to get the joy of seeing them move forward?" The answer was yes—to all of it!

Then I examined the follow-up question of what I was expecting. The answer went something like this: I wanted these kids to say, "Mrs. Lesia, you saved my life and I'm doing better because of you!" I wanted probation to say, "Lesia, you are amazing, and we want an indefinite contract with you to use you in all these different areas . . ." While probation did express their gratitude and respect for me and what I do, my low "success rate" was getting to me. I let what I perceived as failure make me stop doing what I was supposed to do. What was that? To impart the skills needed for success. Whether the kids used them was up to them, not me. Am I sad when they don't make good choices and waste their talent? Of course. But I still must do what I feel I'm supposed to do even if I don't get a "win" or a "thank you," and even if my kids flounder through life. I can't make the story about me: if *I* failed or not, or if *I* get a load of appreciation. The story is about *them* and giving *them* what *they* need.

So, what does a healthy *why* look like? It looks like this: I provide foster care because I love kids and I want to meet their needs the best way I can. Looking at the true *why* and looking honestly at what you expect may not be easy, but it sets you up for a lot less head beating (our own), possibly fewer grey hairs, and a whole lot more inner peace!

LESS IS MORE

We as foster parents and guardians do this because we love to give and because we love. We love the kids, and we love the idea of a safe place. We give of ourselves, we love to give love, and to give the kids what they didn't have. We want the best for them. Sometimes, in all our giving and love we create the opposite of what we hoped for. Instead of happiness, joy, or gratitude, we get anger, frustration, guilt, and feeling overwhelmed. What's that all about? One would think the foster kids would be grateful to be out of an unhealthy situation and into a place of plenty. Well the reality is, that unhealthy place of suffering was the place where their parents and siblings were. It was a familiar place, a place of familiar dysfunction. So when they get into a home where there is an abundance of love, joy, food, and stuff, it's a shock. It brings up emotions and feelings that they may not be used to. They may not know how to react to such love and abundance. Just being able to receive and appreciate what you give them may be something they don't know how to do.

There is nothing worse than feeling overwhelmed. Imagine coming into a new home, new people, new food, and new stuff. That's why I believe that we need to KISS:

Keep It Simple Sweetie! Simple meals, simple guidelines, simple everything. Don't throw lobster and sushi at them on the first day if they are used to eating rice, chicken, beans, and spaghetti. It might sound cool to give them diverse cultural experiences and take them places they've never been. But new things aren't always fun to everybody.

I remember taking one of my foster daughters to the grocery store and saying "What would you like to eat? Pick anything you want." I got the *deer-in-the-headlights* look. Her response was "I don't know. No one has ever asked me what I wanted before." So she picked some chips and juice. She was overwhelmed! Being given too much too fast can stir up questions and emotions like, "Why are they doing this? What do they want back from me? What do I say? Am I betraying my mom or dad if I take these gifts? Will my family think I don't love them?" Then you get the anger: "Why didn't my parents do this for me? Did they even love me? This should be *my* family going on this cruise, not some strangers!" This brings me to my next point.

Go slow in EVERYTHING! Go slow in love, affection, interaction…everything. You may be a hugger, but is your foster child? Have they been abused and don't like to be touched? Are they used to being independent, or are they unaccustomed to family dinners and feel uncomfortable sitting around the table? Go slow. Start with baby steps in everything you do and work your way up.

Ask if you can give them a hug or start with a high-five or a fist bump. My foster daughter (FD) is not affectionate nor does she like to "get into her emotions." So, when something great happens or I let her know how proud I am of her I high-five her. It's our special thing that says, "This is awesome," or "You did great!"

Sometimes it may seem like it's taking forever for things to change, but consider being in your foster child's shoes. For years they've had poor parenting, negative situations, and other traumatic events in their thirteen, fourteen, or sixteen years of life. So being in your amazing, loving home for four months is not long in the foster world. Hang in there. Slow and steady wins the race.

GREAT EXPECTATIONS

From Lesia's Dictionary:

Expectation: a belief that something will happen or is likely to happen; having a preconceived idea or belief about how successful or good someone or something will be and what it will look like or how it will happen.

Expectancy: a feeling that something is going to happen; believing and expecting something to happen without a preconceived idea of what it will look like or how it will happen.

If there is any area where less is more with these kids it's in the realm of expectation. When my kids come into my home I don't expect much, if anything. Hear me: these are kids come in with *baggage,* and it's not Gucci! I don't expect much, but I do expect wonderful things for their lives. How fast, how—or even if—those wonderful things will happen, is a roll of the dice.

Let's look at the definition of *expectation.*

With expectations we have an idea, an image, a picture, already painted in our loving little heads about how everything is going to be. And what I'm saying to you is toss it! All of it! Start with an empty canvas. When we have a belief about how successful or good someone or something will be we set ourselves up for disappointment, frustration, and disillusionment.

Now take the word *expectancy*.

Expectancy, or being expectant, is good! We can anticipate something is going to happen but not have the picture already painted; instead we just let the painting evolve before our eyes one stroke at a time.

I like to observe my foster kids, see where they are emotionally and socially. If they don't know how to wash dishes, say thank you, or be considerate, I make a mental note of things that we need to work on slowly.

If I see that they don't know how to value things like furniture, walls, food, china etc. I certainly take that into consideration. While we would like our kids to have nice things, and they may want wonderful things, I would think twice about it or you could end up with a conversation like this:

Parent: Where are those earbuds I bought you?

Jack: I don't know.

Parent: You do know those cost $150, right? Please look for them!

Jack: Yeah, sure.

(Three days later)

Parent: Did you find those earbuds?

Jack: NOPE!

The next day Jack comes home with a $6 pair of earbuds from the discount store, that he borrowed from his friend.

Parent: Why are you wearing those cheap earbuds? Did you even bother to look for the other ones? I spent a lot of money on those earbuds!

Jack: Yeah, I looked. But nobody asked you to spend that much money. That's on you!

You may be having that type of conversation about anything. You could be saying, "Hey, ketchup bottles don't go on my couch; it costs a lot of money," or, "It takes a lot of work and money to paint my walls. Why are you scuffing them with your shoes?" The list can go on, and their responses can be frustrating. A conversation about valuing things might head off some of these problems at the pass.

You may get some kids who, despite their situation, are very grateful and appreciative. But for the most part these kids have had no "home training." Be wise. Get to know them. If you think they will value nice things, then go for it. If not, then leave that form of giving for another day.

One area that I would like to caution you about is expecting your foster kids to be emotionally present and in touch with their feelings. Emotions to some are like poison. Seriously—if they touch them they could die! Even worse, they may show some sign of weakness, become vulnerable, and have to depend upon and trust someone—God forbid! Showing no emotion is a survival technique. I remember when I told my last FD that I was very ill. She looked at me and said with an emotionless face, "You know I don't do emotions right? So, I want to know how does your sickness affect me?" Translation: "I'm sorry you're sick, but what's going to happen to me?" If I didn't know her history, personality, and social skills I could really have gotten angry and felt hurt because I would have *expected* more compassion and feelings. She didn't come equipped with knowing how to express any emotion except anger, and boy could she express that well!

A conversation sometime soon after a case like I just described might start something like this: "If someone isn't feeling well, what would be a good response?" And then you would work on responses. We all have *expectations*—it's what keeps us hopeful. However, this fostering gig becomes a little more peaceful when we accept our kids with arms wide open, and bring *expectancy,* not *expectations,* to the journey before us.

THEY AREN'T YOUR KIDS

As great foster parents, or *resource families*, of course we love our foster kids like they're our own. But the reality of it is, they're not. This, my friends, is a *must-know*! I have rules and standards for my biological kids that just don't work for fosters. I have to hear my bio kids say to me, "You would never let us get away with doing this or talking to you like that!" My response to them is this: "Hmm… okay. Was your mom physically abusive? Did you have to try and find your own food at age nine? No? Hmmm… Were you taken from your parents because your mom chose the dad who molested you over you? No? Hmmm… Then what are you complaining about again?" Their response: SILENCE (and slight rolling of the eyes).

There is no way that we can expect the same behavior from some foster kids as we do from our own, assuming our own kids behave well. We have rules and guidelines for our children and they are expected to follow them. Remember, with your own kids you instill values, morals, certain expectations, and guidelines from birth. They know how you as parents operate and they know what is acceptable and what isn't. Our foster kids come in blind, so to speak, knowing nothing about us, our rules, our personality—nothing! Usually there are unhealthy reasons that the kids are removed from their home, and they have had to deal with unacceptable behavior. That poor behavior and lack of parental guidance affect the child. Their behavior may be horrible. They may say and do things that you could never imagine, but the reality is that "broken is as broken does."

We get kids that can be out of control or have no idea of what home or rules are like. We can't apply cookie-cutter parenting techniques. We just can't expect them to act like our kids or love us like our kids or do anything like our bio kids; it's an unreasonable expectation and will lead to frustration. Just like each bio child is different, so is each foster child. I have basic requirements in our home: be respectful, do what you're asked, be in at curfew, text and let us know where you are, etc. Even those seemingly basic requests can be a challenge for foster kids. It takes time to learn something new. This is when we parents learn things like patience, and patience, and flexibility, and grace, and patience, and unconditional love, and patience. Oh, and did I mention patience?

Some kids are streetwise and know more about the streets than most adults. So to treat them like kids that aren't street savvy will be frustrating for the kid, and for us as parents. I tell my bio kids to be home before dark, or I meet them at the bus stop. I really panic at the thought of them having to take the bus home from work at night. One of my foster daughters got off work at 8 p.m. I once offered to pick her up and she gave me a look like, "Are you serious?" And she said, "Lesia, I'm not that girl. I'm from the streets, I know what's up and I can handle myself. I'll text you when I'm on my way home." I can handle that compromise. Remember who they are, where they've come from, and that they are not your bio kids— or the foster child you had before. Watch them, learn about them, and trust your gut.

Our job as foster parents is not to become their parents. It is not our job to replace their parents. Our job is to give them a safe place to detox, heal, and rest from trauma. We support them as they try to process what's going on in their life. The goal is always reunification. Reunification doesn't always happen, but it can, and it remains the goal. We are to treat them with love like our own, while knowing they will be going home one day. It's a challenging relationship to balance. Loving *full-out* and then knowing they will be leaving is heartbreaking! Even understanding our role as foster parents doesn't make it easier. Still, we don't have to be totally taken by surprise by all the emotions that come flooding in. Our place in their lives during this time is equally as important as their parents. We are the ones entrusted with these lovelies to keep them safe, to love them, and to help them through probably one of the hardest times in their lives, and care for them as our own. Yeah…that's us!

WE GET BY WITH A LITTLE HELP FROM OUR FRIENDS

There is a wealth of resources available to you, including the social worker, therapist, probation officer, school resources, foster family associations, support groups, family, and friends. Use them, use them, use them! You don't have to do this alone. I make regular calls to my FD's therapist, social worker, school principal, school therapist, and anyone else I know can help. That is what they are there for. Going it alone is a great way to burn out and feel like throwing in the towel. Ask questions, ask questions, ask questions! Sometimes you don't want to be THAT foster parent—you know—the one who calls the social worker, the school, or P.O. (probation officer) all the time and has the reputation of being annoying. You start thinking people are rolling their eyes when they see your number on caller ID. You fear losing your license because it seems like you can't handle it, calling and asking so many questions. But believe me, taking away your license is the LAST thing social services wants to do. Getting clarity, or asking questions that are important to you, is worth being THAT foster parent. Talk to everybody because it's their job to support you and to get you the resources you need. I'm sure they would rather roll their eyes (not that they would) because of your many inquiries than lose a great resource family and have to find another home for the child. Make use of all the opportunities afforded to kids in the foster-care system. Sign them up for sports, art; set up play dates if they are little. Find other teens in your area that may be in foster care, or teens that might be a good influence. Bottom line: the less you have to do the better. Trust me, you'll be a little more relaxed and feel a lot less pressure. Last but not least, make sure you utilize their amazing CASA (Court Appointed Special Advocate) worker. They are Godsends!

Social workers/caseworkers are amazing! Sometimes overworked and overwhelmed, but amazing! I want to say loud and clear that caseworkers are a vital link in the chain of care for foster kids. I believe that it takes a certain very special kind of person to do what they do. Ideally caseworkers partner with parents toward the same goal, and we love them and need them.

Having said that, when there are less-than-ideal lapses in caseworker performance, we must be prepared to step in and do what is best for our foster kids. My first FD was brought to me with two or three hours' notice—yeah sometimes that happens. When she got to our home, the caseworker/social worker helped bring her belongings inside, had me sign some papers, and was just about to walk out the door! She gave me all of twenty minutes of her time. There was no, "Is there anything you need? Do you have questions?" We didn't sit down and discuss her case or anything. I was nervous and in shock. This is the big game, the moment I've trained for, and the coach says, "Here's the ball, I'll be in the locker room." I finally said, "Uhhh…, you do know this is my first placement, right?" She was surprised and then sat down with me and talked for a few more minutes. I'd like to say it got better, but it didn't. We lost contact with her for several weeks with no explanation, no returned phone calls—nothing. After many attempts to reach her, I called a name on one of the forms, which ended up being her supervisor. I told her what happened and she moved quicker than Usain Bolt! She sent all the information I needed regarding our new FD and connected me with support resources. She also let me know that the caseworker left town on emergency leave. There was a breakdown in communication and I was never told or given anyone to contact in her absence. After that point things were handled professionally and apologetically. I received more-than-ample support. The caseworker came back and we discussed what happened, and all ended well. We had many conversations during our time together. We didn't always see eye to eye, but that's okay.

Caseworkers aren't perfect and have their own issues—personal as well as the issues of other children and their families. So, if things aren't going well with your social worker, 1) Give them the benefit of the doubt and extend some grace. Maybe it's a demanding time for them and they are swamped with cases. 2) Make sure to get important numbers and paperwork at the time of placement. If they don't have them then make sure you establish a time for the papers to be sent or have a follow-up call. 3) Be assertive. Don't just let things get out of control, or complain and get angry. Make the calls; send the emails. 4) Call other parents who have been doing the foster care thing. Call support groups or anyone who might be familiar with the system and ask them for numbers, advice, and solutions. 5) If you don't get responses from your caseworker after trying everything then find the supervisor and talk to them. It's what they are there for. They want to keep resource families, and they also want to have a good reputation with the community. The LAST thing they want is for a parent to get into the community bad-mouthing caseworkers and alienating potential foster parents. Put aside pride, fear, emotions, or negative thoughts you may have and do what needs to be done for you and your child.

No one is an island; we need each other. You have a wonderful team to support you, so make the calls and send the emails. You'll be glad you did!

THE ROUND TABLE

The *Round Table* in the legend of King Arthur was designed for people to come together in fellowship as equals for discussion, conversation, listening, and speaking, without any one person taking precedence over the others. I imagine that conversations held at Round Tables throughout history may have prevented many wars! We have a round table in our home, and it's our dinner table. We use this table for our initial meeting with our foster kids, as well as family dinner, and discussions to prevent our own wars. We present our table as a safe place, a place of love and accountability. Our first Round Table meeting with foster kids is spent talking about some of our guidelines to make the living transition smooth. We discuss what our foster kids can expect of us and what we would like from them. Likewise, we give them a chance to express what's on their minds as they enter this new living arrangement, and to ask questions.

Different people handle their initial meeting and welcome into the home differently. We like to talk about things up front, but some like to let their kids feel their way around and discuss issues as they come up. We introduce simple guidelines, like being required to do chores, being clothed properly when walking around the house, coming to family dinner, etc. We let them know that this is their home and that they are welcome to the food in the fridge unless it is marked for someone else. They are free to watch TV within guidelines—these are the sorts of things we bring up initially. (You'll find a full list of our guidelines later in the book.) When we go through the guidelines we give them a written copy of it, though I am uncertain how realistic it is to expect that they will study it. We give them a week to adjust and get acquainted with us, and our house, and then we start to implement chores and other responsibilities. I go over the chores and make sure to show them what I expect as far as cleaning. This is all done with my understanding that I can have all the guidelines I want, but implementation will take time, trial and error, and patience. We also ask our foster kids what they would like from us, what on the list of guidelines they find challenging, and how we can work through it. Usually they say the guidelines are fine, but soon enough we find that there are some challenges. We learn what the kids are capable and not capable of doing, and so we revamp, negotiate, compromise, and extend grace.

From Lesia's Dictionary:

Grace: *cutting our kids some slack, while holding them accountable.*

I had one girl who was a cleaning machine! She was great and loved to clean the kitchen—go figure. Then I had one who was like Pig Pen on Charlie Brown. Her room literally looked like a tornado went through it. That wasn't a battle I really wanted to fight, so the guideline I gave her was that her clothes had to be off the floor. If she wanted them on her bed and on the chair, that was her business—but off the floor. Then she graduated from just off the floor to that plus a thorough cleaning once a week, and if she wanted to go somewhere she had to clean her room. We made sure to clearly define what a "clean room" meant, so there were no questions about what was expected. We also were open for change and negotiation.

We also share guidelines for our home atmosphere, and ways we like to keep it peaceful. What do you do when you get a child whose everyday vocabulary consists of dropping f-bombs and every other cuss word you can imagine? How do you handle it and how do you react? For us, we maintain a cuss-free zone and make that very clear in the beginning. Yes, the implementation of that can be a struggle. With one FD, there were lots of, "Oops, sorry about the f-bomb," or, "Sorry, my bad." And we gave her grace and encouraged her to express herself in more appropriate ways that would be beneficial for her in the workplace and communicating with people other than her *girls* (friends). It took a while but she was eventually able to express her anger and frustration without cussing. Everyone is different in their approach and what is allowed in their home, but the conversations need to happen. Even though there is a variety of ways to handle things, there are some things that remain the same no matter what your style: patience, love, time, and grace.

WE ARE FAMILY

Our desire and passion is to provide a family for our foster kids, to give them some of the things they missed out on: dinner around the table, movie night, food, stability, safety—all that great stuff. What we get instead are teenagers with busy schedules, lots of homework, and only eating together once a week. Not to mention that instead of laughter, joy, and enjoyable conversation, there is silence, awkward staring, and that look of sheer terror. What is going on? Why aren't they excited about being with a "real" family at dinner around the table? Why aren't they thrilled about having a mom who cares and a dad who wants to love and protect them? Why won't they let us parent them? (Remember, they aren't our kids.)

Some foster kids have no idea what family is. *Family* may mean the uncle who molested them. Or the dad that never said, "I love you." The word *family* is relative—no pun intended. The idea of family interaction may be foreign to your foster teens. Simple things like having a conversation, learning how to say hello when they enter a room, even having food in the house, may seem weird to them. Not to mention being told what to do from an adult, especially adults they don't know or trust.

We parents usually come to the foster relationship with an idea of what we want the family to look like. What is more important than what we think it should look like is what our foster kids really want and need. We want to nurture, train, equip, and get them ready for the big world, all in six months to a year! Looking back at myself with such expectations, I'm *ROFL* (rolling on the floor laughing).

We have had four different girls with four unique needs. At first we tried to cookie-cut the concept of family, meaning that in our eyes, all of their family needs were the same and family was what WE envisioned. We assumed all of them wanted family, with a dad and mom and all the stuff we had to offer. My husband wanted desperately to build a relationship with girls, but only one of the four truly wanted that. He bent over backwards to make all four feel welcome, to interact with them, and show love to them. In return he sometimes got rejected, ignored, and rarely talked to. It was hard on him. He was frustrated, disappointed, and angry at times. Why? Because our expectation of what a foster family was all about got shot to heck!

After months of stress and frustration, through a conversation with the girls we figured out what they really wanted and needed. Our relationships drastically changed. Stress levels dropped dramatically, communication was better, and there was a lot more peace for us. We weren't living the ideal family vision, but we weren't in the Titanic either.

Daughter #1 didn't want another family. She desperately wanted to connect with her bio family despite the dysfunction, heartache, and pain she regularly endured with them. Her goal was to make money, save up, and move out when she turned eighteen. So, we tried to meet her needs by talking about budget, opening a bank account, and teaching her life skills without her knowing she was being taught. This worked much better. I can't say it was very successful and she did all the things she said she wanted to do, but we weren't trying to impose our idea of family onto her. It became manageable.

Daughter #2 really loved us all and wanted to stay with us. She embraced my husband as dad, me as mom, and our daughter as the big sister. She thrived on the game night, family dinner, and movie night. When it was time to go, we were all in tears and we keep in touch to this day.

Daughter #3 just needed room and board. Her mother and family were in the picture and she had a plan to graduate high school, get an apartment, and go to college.

We supported her in her plans, hubby helped with homework and whatever else she needed to accomplish her goals. We rarely saw her with all her meetings, school, and other activities. She stuck to her plan and accomplished everything she set out to do. We were so proud of her and we never heard from her again. But that's okay.

Daughter #4 loved the idea of family. She wanted Steve to be her dad, me to be her mom, and even talked about adoption or legal guardianship. She loved us, but the hurt and longing of her family interfered, and she rejected us and even ran away. She was the most challenging in that area. We loved her but didn't push her. We didn't get a chance to figure out what she wanted because she ran away and never came back.

While we met each of their diverse needs, the basic rules and certain family activities of the house still applied, one of those being family dinner once a week. That was a success for all our girls. Build your family dynamics and fun according to their needs. If they want to get ready to move out at eighteen, have a family night and talk about budgeting, apartments, or things that interest them, in a fun, social way. Get creative. However, you must remember that it takes two to tango. If your foster teen isn't willing to participate or accept what you have to offer, then they aren't willing…yet. But keep hope alive!

You don't have to abandon your vision of what family can be as a foster parent. Just be willing to do a little adjusting. Be the family your foster kid needs, and it might just turn out to be the family you want!

TO TRUST OR NOT TO TRUST

That is the question.

Trust: Is it better to start out at 100 percent trust and potentially be disappointed? Or is it better to start at 0 percent trust and make them earn it? This is a difficult question.

How I handle the trust question will be completely different from how you will. Each child is different, and you can sense the attitude, the heart, and the intent of your child, and handle them accordingly. I found that getting as much history as possible on the child is key. Ask about the good, the bad, and the ugly. Use that information to govern how you will approach the child, and the safety of your home and belongings, without judging.

I know—you're asking, "How do you do that?" I can't say I have the answer. But you may learn from my approach: After I gather as much information about the child as I can, I have a conversation with the child. It goes something like this:

"Sarah, I'm so glad you're here, and we want you here. We make it a practice to find out as much about our foster kids as possible, the good and the bad. We've been told that you are smart, artistic, kind, and compassionate.

We've also been told that you have a history of stealing. Is this true?"

If she says yes then I proceed with, "Thank you for being honest. So, do I need to hide all my stuff and keep my purse near me? Here's how we operate: we will give you the benefit of the doubt, meaning every time something goes missing we're not going to assume you took it. We will ask you if you've seen it and we will expect the truth. We would rather have the truth than a lie. Lying will destroy trust in a minute. We will always accept the truth even if you lie at first and come back with the truth. We believe that you want to do better and that you do not want to be known as a thief. We want to help you not to steal. We want to provide the things you need, and if we can't give them to you, to help you find a way to get them without disrespecting yourself and us by stealing. If you lie or steal from us then we will have to go to the next level to ensure that our belongings are safe. We want you to stay safe as well. As of now you have 100 percent of our trust."

Now, I still use wisdom. I may give the benefit of the doubt but I ain't no fool! I will put my purse in my room, keep my jewelry secure and not leave money lying around. While she may want to change, she may not have acquired the skills to resist temptation.

But what if she says, "No, I'm not a thief"? In that case the conversation might go something like this:

"So, your social worker says you have a history of stealing, and you're saying no, you don't. Where did she get that information from? Why would she make it up and how do you explain these incident reports?" She might begin blaming others, like, "The P.O. hates me," etc. "Okay, so you're telling me you're not a thief. Should we trust you, and if yes, why? You say it's not true. We're going to give you the benefit of the doubt; your slate is clean. We will trust you until YOU prove that you are not trustworthy. Trust and honesty are important here. We want to make this work and we believe you do too."

It's okay to be up front and confront them when they have lied or stolen, or whatever the infraction may be. It's okay to implement consequences for their behavior. Bringing up the conversation on trust and telling the truth is important. I always give them a chance to "come clean" or ask questions before I bring up the facts or evidence.

Me: You told me you were at school all day.

Sarah: I was. I went to all my classes.

Me: Then why did I get a call from your school saying you didn't show up?

One major trust question is whether or not to give your foster teen a key to your house. I have always given the kids a key to the house, with strict guidelines. No one is allowed in the house when we aren't home. However, we have experienced catching some of our girls in lies and other questionable events. We really think long and hard about this question, and listen to our "spidey sense." Some foster parents will never give their teen kids a key, and that's okay too, I guess, but it doesn't send a very welcoming message.

I'll give you a little story about the key. One of my girls, age seventeen, was not the most responsible individual. She lost numerous bus passes, ID cards, and other things. One thing she held on to was her door key. One day she informed me that she had lost it and wanted another one. I said no. The reason? Her friends were on the shady side, smoked weed, and stole. I didn't know where my key was and it could be in one of her friend's pockets, and they know where we live (which they shouldn't). They could walk in here and rip us off or trash my house because they had some beef with her.

Since we did not get her a key she had to wait until one of us got home in order to get in the house. She had a bad habit of not keeping her word. She would make a plan, then without telling us, decide to change it and expect us to rearrange our schedule to accommodate her. On several occasions she was caught in the rain, sitting out in the cold and REALLY, REALLY ticked off at me. On those occasions, I told her to go hangout at Starbucks or the library until we got home. This was a lesson in responsibility. She begged me for another key and I said no. I didn't trust where she hung out, and she needed to learn to be more responsible. After about a month of agony and attitude from her, she found her key…under her bed! She learned a few things from that, and she never lost her key again.

If we don't teach our foster kids accountability and personal responsibility they are going to be in trouble in the real world. They can't steal from their job and get away with it, and we need to teach them that.

You may be the first adult that has ever given your foster teen the benefit of the doubt despite their reputation. And believe me, to have someone trust them even though they don't deserve it can make all the difference in the world to them. Some will value that trust and others will take advantage of it. How you handle the trust issue is up to you and your comfort level. Even if they don't have a history of stealing I'm still very wise and cautious, without judging. Lead them not into temptation…so I'll just put my jewelry away for now.

I SEE YOU!

From Lesia's Dictionary:

Transparency: humility; making yourself easily understood; not fake; straightforward; not being afraid to express how you feel or admit that you messed up.

Forgiveness: doesn't mean what they did was okay, right or acceptable—it means you release control of the power the other person has over your life, thoughts, and emotions.

to Forgive: to stop feeling angry at or hurt by someone; to stop feeling resentment against someone who has offended or did you wrong.

Transparency. That's a scary word! We can all appreciate transparency, usually in other people. We want our kids, our spouses, our dogs, and everybody else to be transparent, open, and honest. But us…not so much. Transparency in the parent-child relationship is a new concept. We typically want our kids to share, be open, and admit to being wrong, because that's what kids are supposed to do, right? But how will they truly learn to do that if they don't see it modeled? The traditional mindset regarding parenting is that parents don't apologize, share their feelings, and especially that they don't admit to being wrong. Parents are the authority figure, not a friend or equal. But in reality, being transparent doesn't lessen our position as a parent—it takes it to the next level.

Don't be afraid to be transparent, genuine, and real. I have worked with teens in the juvenile probation system, and their parents, and the one thing I hear them say about their parents or guardians is, "They don't understand," "They don't want to listen," "They think they are always right," and, "All they do is yell and disrespect me." Transparency is something most teens don't see in adults, but it's one of the things that has given me the most success. I am very respected by the kids I work with and my foster kids. Even with my transparency they know that I don't "take no mess," and they certainly know not to mistake my kindness for weakness. My kids don't think I'm weak or soft, or forget that I'm the parent or adult just because I say I was wrong. I have had to apologize many, many times. When I do I keep it simple something like, "Sorry I accused you of taking my five bucks. I found it in my pants. Please forgive me." Or, "Oops, my bad; you were right. Please forgive me." Or, "I'm sorry I yelled at you, please forgive me." In prior generations parenting experts would have called that being weak and not showing your kids who's boss. But that could not be farther from the truth. Kids want to be validated and respected. Acknowledging them is crucial. Don't hesitate to have a conversation about the emotional blow-up or the false accusation or whatever the situation was. Transparency is not weakness, it's being emotionally responsible and validating the child's feelings and experience. Let them learn from your example what it means to be accountable for their actions and emotions.

In case you didn't know, teens can spot a fake a mile away. Trust me, they know *straight up* (up front, right away) if you are judging them or have preconceived ideas about them. One thing you can't get away with is being phony. Teens even know if you're being *low-key* (kind of, a little) phony. So, to thine own self be true, and get real with your judgments, expectations, and phoniness.

One thing I find important is to ask for forgiveness. It's very important to say, "Please forgive me," and make sure they say the words "I forgive you," or at least work toward it. Many foster kids carry unforgiveness. Helping them to become accustomed to forgiving can help bring healing from their past, present, and future wounds.

My friends, *transparency* is not a four-letter word— it's a twelve-letter word. When we parent with transparency we really are parenting *like a boss* (cool and in charge).

JUDGING AMY . . . JUAN . . . ADIJA . . .

The word *teen* can strike fear into the heart of the toughest person. Add on the words *foster care*, and some will run screaming like a crowd in a bad Godzilla movie!

There is no doubt that teens have a reputation for being rude, disrespectful, hormonal, and scary individuals. And those are all verifiable descriptions. Anyone who has been around a teen has experienced at least a little bit of it. But that doesn't mean that ALL teens are going to be like that, or stay like that forever.

We have already discussed gathering as much info as possible about your foster teen so that you have an idea of the person you're getting. We've discussed the difference between expectation and expectancy. Now let's discuss what happens when we've learned some things about our teens that cause us to expect behaviors from them. It might be tempting to get so locked into the negatives you've been told about the child that you don't notice them making small changes for the better. Everyone is capable of changing. Maybe somewhere between the last foster home and yours, your foster teen had an epiphany. We don't know what is going on in their heads. All they may need is the right environment to change for the better. What if your home is that right environment? And what if you are stuck on what was said by others—on the experience of the last foster homes, or the stigma about teens—such that you miss the opportunity to sow positive seeds into their lives and see a glimpse of an amazing young person wanting to change? Life in the foster care tends to move sloooow—tortoise slow. Just because you don't see big changes, don't give up. Even something as small as them saying "thank you," when before they would have just walked off without a kind word, is an indication that they are taking baby steps forward.

I guess what I'm trying to say is give 'em a chance. Use wisdom and take into consideration what you've been told, but also keep an open mind that they can change.

When planning for your foster teen, gather as much valuable information as you can, and when you interact with them bring up the good stuff. They get their faults thrown in their faces all the time and I believe that sometimes they hear it so much they begin to act on it. I hear it all the time: "They already think I'm a thief so why not?" What if they constantly heard people say how smart they were or that they can be anything they want to be?

What an enormous difference that could make! There is a saying that goes, "speak what you want to see happen," so if we consistently speak to the strengths instead of to the weaknesses of our foster kids, there is no telling how things can change and what it could do to that wounded soul.

Use wisdom. If a child has a history of stealing, please don't say, "I've been speaking what I want to see happen," and then leave your valuables out—that's not wisdom. But we all deserve a fresh start, and even when we get one we might blow it. That's where *grace* (cutting some slack while still holding accountable) kicks in and we can give our foster kids a second, third, fourth chance. Don't count them out. It may be that a year into being in your home, or even after they leave your home, the light switches on and they get it. How long did it take some of us to get it? How many of us are still trying to get it?

A person who can look past the obvious and see the possibilities is a beautiful person to be and a wonderful person to share with these lovelies.

COLOR BLIND

I hear people say, "I don't see color." That's a nice statement and I understand where they are going with it. But the truth is, there is color—it's all around us and we must recognize it. In foster care we will get all kinds of color, nationalities, cultures, beliefs, and religions. We must be culturally aware in dealing with the kids that come into our home. For some, looking an adult in the eyes is considered disrespectful. Some kids would prefer beans instead of Chicken Parm. Others may not be "touchy feely" because outward affection is not part of their culture. Or they may want to celebrate a certain holiday that we are not accustomed to. We may not agree with the differences but we can respect them and accommodate them as much as possible. We can do simple things that say, "I honor you and your culture, and I'm not trying to make you forget who you are and be like me."

One of the simple things you can do to show you value their culture is let them be the expert. Ask questions and listen to the answers. Ask your foster teen to cook something or share something about their heritage with your family.

We had Latina girls and they were very up front about what our differences were. Once a month I would take the girls to our local Mexican food store, give them a budget, and let them get the foods they were used to eating. There was lots of Mexican candy and Takis. If you don't know what Takis are, look them up. We each had one week a month to cook dinner and we had some great Mexican food. I made it clear that if they wanted Mexican food they would need to cook it or teach me how, because I don't know how to cook authentic Mexican food. They got a kick out of showing me the ropes!

If your teen isn't forthcoming with information, ask the social worker, or the parent if you have that opportunity, what they like and what are some cultural differences. If there are practices or beliefs that you are not comfortable with then there needs to be a discussion with everyone involved: the social workers, the teen, the CASA etc., to see how things can be worked out. You need to be comfortable in your home, and finding the balance is the key. Get clear in your own mind beforehand about what you are comfortable with, what you will allow, and what you won't allow, and let the caseworker know.

There are basic household rules that will be in place regardless of culture or ethnicity. Speaking with respect is a must no matter where you come from. What respect looks like needs to be discussed because it looks different to different people. Having open and honest conversations about things is essential, because in the foster care world, silence is not always golden.

JUST DO YOU, BOO!

"Just do you, boo!" All the kids were saying it. And what it means is that it doesn't matter what people say about you, what they think about you, or how they treat you. You gotta do you and be you no matter what the *haters* (those who are jealous and don't want you to succeed) say or do! I mentioned before how my husband was dissed, rejected, and ignored by one of our girls. He had a choice to either shut down and reject them because they rejected him, or continue being the kind, giving man that he is. We felt our girls needed to see that no matter how rude they were, and how disconnected they were, that we would not change. We would not stop caring or being who we are: kind, compassionate, honest, etc. Many foster kids have seen people love them when they behave, but reject them when they don't. We have to be different.

I encourage you to continue to attempt to make a connection without being too pushy. Ask how your foster child's day was, talk about little stuff that interests them. Always say hello and good night. Acknowledge an accomplishment and even give some correction. Being aware of their current mental state and emotions can help you figure out when to engage, and when to back out. Remember a few weeks, months, or even years of kindness may not break their hard shell or resistance. But consistency, unconditional love, and meeting their needs might. Continue to be you. Don't let their personal trauma change who you are. They really, really need that emotional stability. Don't lose you; stay true to who you are. "Just do you, boo!"

I DON'T LIKE YOU!

What happens if your foster kid doesn't like you? You like him or her, but he or she just doesn't like you. There are a few things to consider in determining if you're really in an "I don't like you" situation.

Have you had enough time to get to know each other? Sometimes we as adults take time to warm up to people—how much more these kids who have been taken from their home, along with all the other baggage they carry. Adjusting to new rules, atmosphere, "housemates," and home environment is a huge adjustment. Is it a personality issue? Some of you may be super bubbly and full of joy, while your foster child may be mellow. Or the home may be very quiet and they are bubbly, or any of the myriad possible personality variations. This is a good time to step back and get to know your child. See what their likes or dislikes are, how they interact, etc. If they prefer a mellow atmosphere then be prepared to dial it back a little. You don't have to stop being you, but you could be you at a five instead of a ten. Maybe in time you may reach a happy medium and grow to like each other. Another possibility could be that either the foster parent or the foster child is trying too hard. We all have been around someone who just wants to impress people and goes overboard. Instead of impressing people they become super annoying! Take it easy, just relax, and let things flow.

Could your foster child's behavior be a sign of independence, or survival instincts instead? Things like not eating, refusing money, not interacting or accepting help, aren't always a sign of rejection. Your foster child may just be afraid to trust, and therefore they "look out for number one" because the adults in their lives have failed so miserably. That way, the only one they need to rely on is themselves, and they are spared hurtful disappointment. They sometimes make it a point not to accept anything from you because WHEN YOU FAIL— and they know you will—they can still take care of themselves and not suffer any disillusionment. Even with all the love foster parents have to offer, trust takes time. The good thing is that your foster child will trust you as much as they can. I believe they want to make their life with you work well, but there are so many voices screaming at them from the inside, and that makes trust a challenge. Asking for help, for needs, for love, is hard for them to do. We have to be proactive in asking them if they need anything or just saying "Here is five dollars for lunch," instead of, "Would you like five dollars for lunch?"

It may take a while for them to say yes, and it may take a while for them to even be willing to eat your food. Leave snacks and fruit and things they can grab independently. One of my girls would say, "I'm not hungry," or eat just a tiny bit. Then after we were in bed we would hear her in the kitchen getting food. She was afraid that we would say she ate too much. She didn't know how much she was allowed to eat. She also wanted to show her independence and made it a point to let us know she didn't need us. Foster teens are entering a whole new world and every aspect of their lives has changed. Some of them have lived by "hustling" and doing whatever it takes to get what they need. Your job as a foster parent is to respect and understand their situation, and at some point, have a conversation about it.

"Is this the right fit?" This is probably the hardest question we may have to ask. Sometimes things just don't work out and they must find another placement. Before that even becomes an option caseworkers will do their best to provide you with every available resource to make the placement work. Be very open about your concerns and how it impacts you, the family, and the child. Sometimes there are behaviors that you are not willing to tolerate. Know what those are before you take a child. Asking about the child's behavioral issues and history

BEFORE you take them is important. Knowing your limits or your criteria for a child coming into your home could save a lot of time and heartache. Don't forget, you are not obligated to say yes every time they call you about a child. Say yes to the child that will be the best fit. You and your family are your priority. If your family does not remain healthy then no one benefits or is helped. Sometimes the problem is an easy fix and sometimes it isn't. We always want things to turn out okay but they don't always. Sometimes there are things we can do and sometimes there aren't. Do the best you can and remember family first.

WHAT'S WITH THE ATTITUDE!?

Have you ever had one of those days? Those days where everything goes wrong and we get grouchy, we cop attitudes, *mean-mug* people (give dirty looks), or even shut down and retreat? Now, if adults have bad days, imagine not just having one of those days but *one of those lives!* Imagine being a teen with no coping or social skills. Throw in hormones and peer pressure and a messed-up home situation, and yeah—they almost deserve the right to have an attitude! Foster teens are sometimes emotionally drained from having so much to deal with at such an early age—it's not fair and it's not right. If they've got attitude, it is more of a symptom of a problem than the problem itself. The young person's attitude is a sign that something is going wrong in their world, whether it is real, imagined, or otherwise.

There is a saying about walking in the other person's shoes. That will come in handy in understanding and empathizing with them. I'm not saying that it's okay to accept poor behavior and just empathize all the time, because that does nothing to help them out in the real world. Instead, I'm suggesting that you don't take their attitude personally, because it may not have anything to do with you. It could be the inner turmoil and thoughts swirling around in their undeveloped minds. Again, patience, and patience, and flexibility, and grace, and patience, and unconditional love, and patience.

One of my foster kids had been really *attitudinal* for a week. I mean like on a scale of one to five she was a five and a half! Here she was, walking in the house without speaking, treating my husband like he doesn't exist, yelling, and talking back to me in a rude way. Not cool. I knew something was going on inside. Everything in us wanted to jump on it and say, "Don't you come into our house with that attitude! We don't have to put up with this so you better get your act together!" But I had to go back to my baseline thought that this girl is broken due to no fault of her own. I couldn't expect her to behave normally—with respect, consideration, politeness, etc. She missed out on learning the basic skills needed to function in a healthy way.

Some foster teens are just plain ticked off. When I remind myself of that, I don't get as angry. Instead I become empathetic and sad that kids so young have been through so much. That's the moment to extend a little grace.

One day my FD was running late for school, which doesn't fall under the "grace" category. She looked bad—

tired, beat up emotionally, and just dragging. This tended to happen after extended time with mom, and not taking her meds. This opened the door for me to say, "You look exhausted and emotionally beat up." I sat her down and shared what I saw, which was depression, frustration, and anxiety. I told her how sad it was to witness all that she has to think about at such a young age. She explained through tears how mentally tired she was and how the stresses of life and the thought of moving out at eighteen were causing her anxiety and making her want to use drugs. She shared that dealing with her mother's depression, feeling responsible for it, and trying to fix everybody had her worn out.

That day I gave her permission to stay home. I had to look deeper than what was manifesting. There was more to it than her just being a pain in the rear with her attitude. The saying, "You can't judge a book by its cover" has never rung truer than with our foster kids.

RUNAWAY CHILD,
RUNNING WILD

I know what it's like to experience a runaway foster child. The incident brought me a whole new set of *why?* and *what?* to explore: Why did she run away? What did we do wrong? Was our love for her not enough? Did we do enough to accept her and care for her? What do we do when she gets back?

Then the fear kicked in: Where in the world is that girl? Is she okay? Am I going to lose my license? Is her mom going to kill me? Then came the anger: What the heck is she thinking? How rude and inconsiderate!

Here's how it all went down: She lied and said she was going to the mall with a friend she met at a work-study program a few weeks earlier. I knew the new friend's parents and I had met the friend as well. She did go to a mall but not our local one. Instead she went to a mall in the big city not far from our town.

She saw some old friends she used to stay with and decided she didn't want to come home. After the first day away, the fear, guilt, and condemnation set in and she didn't want to come back at all for fear of our reaction. She was gone for three days.

But why? Why stay gone when we hit it off so well and she really liked it here?

She was afraid to come home because in the past she was judged, ridiculed, and punished when she did something wrong. That's what her dad and mom did, and that's what she expected from us too. It was the longest three days of my life.

Here's how we handled it: After she was gone for four hours past her curfew, at about 12:00 a.m., and after numerous calls to friends, neighbors, and parents of the new friend she went to the mall with, we called the CFS emergency number and reported her missing. Then we called the sheriff's office to file a missing persons report. The sheriff's office came and took the report and then we waited…and waited. I'm told that most law enforcement agencies don't take reports until seventy-two hours have passed. However now, because of the recent rise in human trafficking, they don't waste any time.

Here's what happened when our "missing person" got home: She walked in the house—with an attitude mind you! I was in the kitchen beckoning her to come to me. She refused, but I persisted. I smiled and said, "Come here." As she came to me I embraced her and she sobbed. I wanted her to know that we loved her no matter what she did. Again, each child is different and needs to be approached differently. This girl needed love, and that's what we gave her. After that she was grounded for two weeks and we gave her a journal and questions that she had to answer each day, about her goals, what she felt when she was gone, what caused her to run away, and how her thoughts and mindset might need to change. She understood the worry and concern she had caused us. She said she was sorry and asked us to forgive her. And all was right in the world again.

That is, at least for two weeks, when she ran away again. This time it was overnight to her boyfriend's house. We went through the same procedure, notifying everyone. Again she was grounded, and we took her phone and said no TV. She did a lot of reading! She finished her first book ever and it was over one hundred pages. She finally understood and decided not to run any more. This was where she wanted to live forever, and make us her forever home. It was great and we were happy for about a month…and then, guess what. She ran away again, and this time she didn't come back. Her social worker and therapist located her and said she didn't want to come back because we were mean and my husband looked at her weird—this from the girl who went jogging with my husband and ran up the stairs to the *Rocky* theme, celebrating their jogging/walking victory.

We found out that this was her pattern. She was a "runner," a chronic runaway, and she created fictitious dialogues and scenarios to confirm and validate her behavior and give herself reasons to run.

We were willing to give her one more chance with very strict stipulations, but her social worker and CASA worker felt that for the safety of our family she should not return to our home, and we reluctantly agreed.

Did we fail her? Did we do something wrong? What happened? In this case, I think we did everything too right. I think the basic desire for and resentment of her bio family was deeper than we knew. Even though she wanted to live with us, the pain of not having that in her own blood relatives was more than she can handle. The "perfect" family was too much for her, and her *emotional detox* brought up difficult feelings, revealing some unresolved mental health issues. Three months of love and acceptance will not magically erase years of trauma. Sometimes we just can't help them, and sometimes we just can't save them, particularly if they don't want to be helped or saved. We can only hope that something was said or done that they can cling to later on. We can only hope that they will get it together one day.

Here's how it stands today: We eventually heard from our FD through her CASA via email saying that she was sorry for running, and for the pain she had caused. She was grateful for the love we showed her in caring for her. She said that she loved us. She was finally placed in the home of a relative whom she loved, which is what she'd always wanted. I wish I could say that she's doing well, but she ran away from her relative's home too, and has not been found. She is now eighteen, her case has been closed, and no one knows where she is.

My family went through a lot of post-runaway evaluation. It's okay to ask yourself the tough questions in any situation, whether it is an argument, a runaway, or a terminated placement. Once you've asked and answered the questions, acknowledge it, make amends, make the changes, and move on. Sometimes things are so deep that it takes God himself to heal the wounds. Remember that we are foster parents not foster perfects.

TORN BETWEEN TWO MOTHERS

One of the things I've noticed is the extreme guilt that foster children carry. They feel guilty for leaving their parent even though it isn't their fault—they just feel guilty. They feel guilty for liking the new home and parents, for receiving love and food from people other than their family. That's why I say they are torn between two mothers. The loyalty to dysfunction is unbelievably strong. You would think that they would run into the arms of safety, right? Yeah...not so much. The guilt might take the form of rejecting you, anger, disengaging, or acting out, just to name a few. While we are trying to be the good guy, we end up being the bad guy, the enemy, the one who ripped them from their family. One of the biggest things we must do is make it clear to our foster kids that we are NOT trying to take their parents' place. We acknowledge their feelings and their loyalty. For younger kids, we let them know that we are just keeping them safe until their mom or dad can take them back (if that's the case). Find out what they find fun about mom or dad, and talk about that. For teens, it is a matter of acknowledging that we aren't their parents and don't pretend to be, and showing respect in the way we talk about their parents, even though what those parents did could have been absolutely horrible! I had a daughter whose mom was certifiably insane! She was verbally abusive and manipulative. She went out of her way to bring guilt and condemnation upon this girl and to get her confused about everything, especially us. We had one set of standards for her, and her mother had other unhealthy standards for her and allowed her to do things that were not acceptable. I had known my FD for at least a year and a half before she came into my home. I was her life coach through juvenile probation, so we had history. I was the one she called when she was upset or in a jam. We had a very close relationship and I was her "other mother." There came a tug of war, and I had to let her know that she was in MY house and certain of her behaviors were not acceptable. I told her that if her mother was not going to abide by our curfew and rules then we were going to talk to her P.O. about my family's safety as it related to her mother's visits. She wanted her mother in her life. She wanted her mother's love and approval, and went along with mom's program for a while. After I laid down the law and said no to this behavior, she was forced to choose between living in our home with our rules, and behaving as her mom was telling her to do. She chose to continue living with us and our rules, and told mom that if she didn't cooperate she would not be able to see her. I'll throw this in too: her mom absolutely hated me! I mean seriously hated me and blamed me for all her problems, and accused me of brainwashing her daughter against her. She would yell at her daughter and say that she defended me too much and ask why she always took my side. Can you imagine what the daughter was going through? She finally caught on that her mom was trying to get her to do things that would get her kicked out of my house. I know…*SMH!!* (shaking my head).

During this whole period I was very respectful and said things like, "Your mom does what she does because she was hurt too, and it's all she knows." "I know what your mom said was hurtful and I want you to know it's not true." After months of watching her come back to our home as a total mental and emotional wreck after seeing her mom, I put my foot down and got real. My daughter knew that her mom had issues, and would say she was crazy, mentally ill, sick, and abusive—that is, all the things I wanted to say but could not as a foster parent because I was trying to be respectful. I finally told her how her mother's behavior was affecting her, that her mom was not healthy, and that I was going to talk to her parole officer about visits. The P.O. saw the constant damage that was done after visits with the mother, and told mom she was no longer able to have visits until she got therapy. Mom made very little effort to get therapy. She went twice and then quit. Even while watching my girl have a nervous breakdown at the hands of her mom, I had to keep my cool. I was enraged and wanted to call that mom and give her a taste of her own medicine. Believe me, her mom did not want the "crazy ghetto chick" in me to come out! She hasn't been out in over thirty-something years, but when it comes to my kids, that scary mama bear could be ready to come out in a minute. As much as I wanted to let her out, I couldn't, and I didn't. If I had let that happen, then this poor girl would have had two "crazy" moms.

Even after this entire episode, our foster daughter maintained an allegiance to her mother. It took many painful interactions with her mom for her to accept the unhealthiness of the relationship and begin distancing herself from her mom, and she finally began to heal. She is no longer in my home, but comes to visit, talk about her problems, get advice (which she doesn't follow), and bring me flowers. She doesn't have much contact with her mom and mom doesn't contact her either. As parents, it's hard to watch when our foster kids' bio families aren't healthy, but they long for those families and they keep hope of going back to what we may feel is a less than optimal place. Just know that although you are not their biological parents, you will always have a unique and special place in their hearts, whether they admit it or not. Loving them, respecting their parents, and protecting them as much as we can is all we can do. In the end, they really aren't our children, even though it feels like they are.

SO, WHAT ARE YOU TRYING TO SAY?

Communicating with teens can be like speaking to someone in a foreign country. You don't speak the same language. You're talking but they just stare at you with a blank look on their faces, shaking their head "no," and making "I don't know" gestures with their hands. That's because you don't know their language and they don't know yours. I see this with teens all...the...time. When young people are little they talk all the time, to the point that you kind of wish they would be quiet. Once they reach that dumbfounding adolescent teen stage, things can go silent. Our job as parents is to figure out ways to keep the lines of communication open and maintain some sort of relationship.

We must learn their language and they must learn ours. We also should consider what the language barriers might be, such as learning challenges or comprehension issues. The challenge for us is to get to know our kids. What do they respond to? What offends them in the way we talk? Can they take being spoken to in a straightforward manner, or do they need the gentle touch? This is the time when the arts of listening, patience, and understanding come in handy.

Let your foster teens know they have the freedom to talk to you about anything, and that you won't retaliate or get angry if they express something negative. You won't flip out if they say they don't like lasagna, or the detergent makes them itch. Let them know you won't judge them and their opinions. Most of the time they won't want to make waves, out of fear that they may get in trouble or be sent to another home. I had one girl who would never say she didn't like something. She would just go with the flow because in her home, her parents would get mad at her if she spoke up. We had to reassure her that we were not going to do that. Our actions had to speak louder than our words.

When giving instructions it is important to be very clear. For instance, "Joey one of your chores is to clean the bathroom once a week on Wednesday. This is how we would like it done." We like to write instructions down for them. We show them how it's done, then we let them do it, and then we check it. When we check their work, we make it a positive experience so they don't think we are criticizing them or judging them. We point out the good things and say, "Looks good, just a little more Windex on the mirror to get those streaks out and it will be fine." As time goes on and they trust us we can be a little more straightforward.

Since we don't know what communication was like for them at home we cannot assume anything. An important question to ask is, "What did you hear me say?" This is very important if the conversation begins to escalate. Their minds go all over the place, so be clear not just in the actual words, but in the intent behind the words. By the same token, we ask them the same question in reverse: "This is what I heard you say; is that what you meant?"

Sometimes we may feel like we need to say everything right now. Things may be escalating and you feel you must get your point across. Well, what we need to say may be important, but so is timing. Saying everything you have to say when things are heated or attitudes are— well— *funky*, may not be the best strategy to make your point. Wait until things calm down and they will be more likely to listen. Your goal is for them to hear what you have to say, so if that means waiting until the next hour or the next day then do that. There is a time for everything.

Nothing is more crucial to your relationship with your foster teen than listening. Listening will take you a long way with teens and is the number one way to communicate with them. Teens need to be heard, and if they feel they aren't being heard they will shut down fast. All hopes of a relationship and conversation could be lost until you prove to them that they are valued, respected, and heard. My relationships with my foster kids and kids in juvenile probation have all been successful because I listen. I listen to a lot of nonsense too, but by listening I am able to let them know that I value their voice, their opinion, and how they feel. They know I listen to understand, and listen without judgment. As I gain their trust I am able to be more and more straightforward and honest about what I hear, without passing judgment. Listening is truly an art that our society has lost. But we can find it again and model it for the young people that come through our doors. #Ihearyou

R-E-S-P-E-C-T

There is a book that I highly recommend called *Parent As Coach* by Diana Sterling. It's the book that totally revolutionized the way I parent. In the book, Sterling did a survey of teens and found out what teens want. The top two things are to be listened to, and respect. Now, we old-school moms and dads are not expected to respect our kids—they are supposed to respect us! They do what we say without question. They do it "because I said so!" But now we are in a whole new era. Kids these days want to know why, and if the answer is good enough they will possibly do what you ask. The other reason they may do what you asked is because they respect you. It's not easy to gain the respect of most young people, especially the ones we get. I've worked with kids in juvenile probation for years and the one thing I have found is that if you don't respect them they won't respect you. By respect I mean acknowledging them as human beings with common sense (though that may be questionable), valuing their opinion, not treating them like they are stupid (though their actions may justify that assumption), and listening to what they have to say without judgment. This also includes speaking to them in a respectful manner. Don't yell at them or talk down to them. This is ironic, because most of them regularly disrespect adults, foster parents, and their friends. But God forbid we *come at them sideways* (with an attitude). I can count on one hand the times I've yelled at the teens I've worked with. Now, my own kids back in the day? All the time. I'm a recovering scream-aholic! Thankfully, I've grown as a person and have learned to keep my peace. My success in building relationships with teens is based on mutual respect. I always tell them how much I respect them, as well as how proud of them I am. "I respect you for going to school when all your friends ditched." Teens, whether in the probation system, foster care, or just plain ol' teens, want to be treated humanely and not like they are rebellious, stubborn, disrespectful kids (which they can be). So, a little respect goes a long way with anybody, but especially teens.

R-E-S-P-E-C-T. Find out what it means to teens.

ME FIRST!

Have you flown on an airplane? Do you remember this statement during the flight attendant's opening announcements: "In case of emergency, put the oxygen mask on yourself first, and then help the one next to you." To most of us that sounds selfish. I want to make sure my child next to me is safe and can breathe! BUT! What if I do that and by the time the baby is okay, I pass out? The same goes for foster parents/resource families. We do what we do because we have a lot of love and compassion, and we are givers and protectors. But if we are not careful to put the oxygen mask on ourselves, our bio family, and our home first, we could pass out and all that love and compassion is pointless. Our family comes first. We must make sure things are going well with our personal relationships, our bio kids, spouses etc., because once the foster kids say, "Adios amigos," you and your family will be back staring each other straight in the face. Hopefully when that moment comes you won't be exchanging looks of burnout, but looks that say, "Yes, we did it!" If you feel this placement is causing too much stress on your family, talk about it with the team—the social worker, CASA worker, and anyone else involved. Sometimes it's an easy fix and sometimes it's not. You can bring a child into your home, give them all the love, food, attention, and video games he could ever imagine, but he or she doesn't have to receive it. You may sometimes have to think about the unthinkable: releasing the placement. If you must say goodbye to the child so you can rest, regroup, and reevaluate, that is not a failure. Letting your home and family fall apart is not success. Remember that your family is number one. Put that mask on yourselves first!

What happens if things are not working out because of their behavior? What if they are causing major problems? I say MAJOR because in every case there will be problems, and fostering teens will change things in your home, either in a good way, a bad way, or maybe both. But if you are being physically and emotionally worn out, you have reached out to your support team, have implemented their suggestions, and have exhausted everything you know to do, it might be time to make the difficult call and give notice of termination of placement. Nobody wants to make that call. Nobody wants to feel like a wimp or a failure.

That's how I felt when I had to make the call for my last FD. In my case, I had become ill. This girl was eight and a half on a scale of ten in measuring neediness. Dealing with her and all her needs was more than I could handle, and the stress was contributing to my physical health challenges. I loved this girl like my own daughter. I'd known her for about three years and was her life coach/mentor before I became her foster mom. I kept trying to keep up with all her emotional needs, talking to her teachers, making sure she didn't violate probation, keeping up with her therapy sessions, and witnessing her drama. There came a point when I just couldn't do it anymore. We decided after months of praying and talking that we had to make the call. Needless to say, she was upset and spiraled out of control for a few days. She pleaded with us to stay because she didn't want to leave, saying this was her home. I was heartbroken. Working with at-risk youth is what I do; I'm used to working with their trauma and drama, and I have never given up on one! But then it felt like I had given up. Yet I couldn't see how could I help her if I wasn't able to take care of myself. I had to put the oxygen mask on ME so that I could get better, and then I could help more kids. More importantly I needed to be healthy in order to take care of my family.

This turn of events made me sad and depressed. I was angry at being ill and feeling like a quitter. Just when I was super low I had a conversation with my FD about my illness and asked her how she felt about the whole situation. She said, "I was frustrated and angry. I know you're probably feeling bad because you love to help young people and you're probably thinking, 'I failed this girl!'" By that point my tears were welling up. She continued, "I am where I am because of you. I got my first job with you. I go to school every day because of you. This is not your fault. You didn't know you were going to be sick. This is not on you. So, all that guilt and stuff, you can just put that to the side." By then I was a sobbing mess. She got up and said, "I'm a go outside, I'll be back by curfew." I don't think she could handle all the tears and emotion, so she had to *bounce* (leave).

I felt so much better after that conversation. If I had not initiated it, I would have continued feeling guilt and thinking she hated me. She also probably needed to say what she was feeling about my illness, and the changes that were about to come. Yay for conversations! Things don't always go smoothly when we open the door to conversation. Our kids may be angry when they leave, and we may feel like we failed them, but we must put that breathing mask on ourselves first, so that we may better help them. With a little time to gain perspective, we can see that no matter how long or short a time they were in our homes, we gave them a safe place to live for that period, and lots of love. And one thing I do know is that love never fails.

TILL DEATH DO US PART

One of the main things that my husband and I discovered in the process of fostering is that our most important relationship is with each other. It doesn't matter how passionate you are about caring for foster kids—that cannot be your number one relationship. Your significant other is at the top of the list of your relationships.

Having lots of conversations and being in agreement with some basic guidelines for the home with your significant other before you have these lovelies in your home is critical. Come to agreement about discipline, consequences, chores, and cell phone communication, among other things. Ask each other if it is okay for your foster kids to eat in the living room. What time is curfew? What's the protocol for friends—do you have to meet them? May friends spend the night? Any and everything that you can think of needs to be talked about and agreed upon with your significant other because, believe me, they will try to divide and conquer! My natural kids used that tactic as well, so why would I imagine that children who have not always been in a healthy atmosphere would not do it?

We had a situation where one foster daughter wanted to go get some chips. She called me and asked if she could go, not telling me that my husband had already said no. Her intent was to go back and say, "Lesia said yes." That, my friends, is called *splitting*. One of the things we did to stop that was to start a group text for any and every correspondence that we had with our girl. That way we made sure that there was no confusion. This wasn't a perfect solution, but it helped.

Unity with your significant other is an absolute must. The two of you must present a united front to your foster child, no matter what. Even if you disagree, don't do it in front of the child. Take it behind closed doors. That includes disapproving looks or body language. Kids, especially teens, can smell disunity a mile away and will use it to their advantage. I hear you saying, "Not my sweet little *snooky-wooky*—she would never do that!" It might sound mean, but twenty years of experience working with teens compels me to say that some of them are like hyenas looking for the weakest prey—I mean it! Show a little weakness, fear, or disunity in your marriage and you'll be on the menu. Ask any teacher, youth leader, parent, or guardian of a teenager and they will agree.

Keep the lines of communication between you and your partner open and frequent. If situations come up that you haven't talked about or are not sure about, consult your partner before you make a commitment. It's easy enough to say to your teen, "Let me talk to —— and I'll get back to you." There is no relationship more important than the one between you and your partner. If you can't see eye to eye, then at least agree to end the day agreeing to disagree. Coming up with a strategy to fix a situation the same day is optimal, but not always doable. But by all means, don't "check out" on your significant other, even if you find that there are constant disagreements, or if you feel that the other is more capable to handle the situation. It's not true. You are needed! Fostering is too much for one person to handle with the other just sitting it out on the couch. Checking out brings a whole new set of problems.

After having numerous, and I mean NUMEROUS, conversations about things we disagreed on, those talks with my husband have paid off! We are still married and still in love. The love for your foster kids is deep, but not as deep as the relationship you've built with your partner. Hang in there and keep communication alive, but more importantly, keep love alive!

FAITH THAT MOVES MOUNTAINS

I am including this section on faith because there are a lot of foster families and future foster families that have strong Christian belief, as I do. We always hear the phrase "separation of church and state." We are told that we mustn't express our faith in this place or in that situation. Yet for those of us who live by faith—regardless of which religion we may belong to—that aspect of our life is very much a part of our fostering process. I do not discriminate and I will not discount you on the basis of your faith—I simply wish to spend a moment sharing my story, and how the life of faith works for me, my household, and the kids that come into it.

Sometimes things get so crazy for me that I put my own self on a timeout! I need to escape by myself, pray, meditate, and just breathe. The behavior, pain, and tragic circumstances of foster kids sometimes strike me as so dismal and hopeless that I can hardly take it. My faith and connection to God is the source that enables me to see these kids' futures, to have confidence in who they can become, and to treasure who they really are, regardless of their behaviors.

Prayer has helped me to keep hope alive when it looks like our kids are certainly heading down a road of destruction and chaos. It's in times like these that I recall the promises of God for their lives and speak that over them. I can say, "Anna, you are talented and I can see the compassion that you have for people. I can see that you have a heart for the underdogs and you will go to bat for them. I want to encourage you to go to bat for them in a positive way. Don't waste your ability to help by helping them do the wrong thing." These are the sorts of insights that I naturally see and assurances that I receive through prayer. Sometimes I find myself telling my kids things that no one could have known, and they are shocked. They always ask me how I know. My response is something like, "Do you really want to know? Yes? Okay. I prayed and that's what God spoke to me about you."

I know some of you don't believe that God exists, and certainly some of you would consider it a stretch to imagine that He speaks to us. Only schizophrenics think they hear God's voice, right? If you do not believe God exists, that's your business, and I don't judge you for that. I'm just talking about how things work for me. I know it may be different for you. There might be others of you who are encouraged to hear that you can take your concerns before God, call out to Him in times of need, and wait expectantly knowing that He has heard you and will respond somehow. If anything will bring you to the farthest limits of yourself, it is fostering teens. What a relief we don't have to bear the burdens of this challenging relationship without divine help!

You, see, I believe that we all were created for a purpose. And no matter what the circumstances surrounding our birth, we are not accidents, *oops*'s or mistakes. We have a purpose and a role in this life that no one else can fill. Life's challenges, traumas, and poor choices can derail us from our purpose—from the peace and abundant life that God originally planned for us. Most foster kids have been derailed. For me, I feel responsible to find out the remarkable things God has planned for these precious children, and to discover who they really are underneath their hard exteriors. I want to let them know that it's not too late for them, and that they can have a second, third, tenth chance. I don't push my faith on the kids that come to live in my house—I simply live my faith. I do invite them to church with me, and if they are old enough to choose not to go then we make other plans for them. I do let them know about my faith, how much God loves them, and how much I pray for them and their destiny. I let them know that I believe God hears and cares enough to answer my prayers concerning them. I have never had a child in my home or that I worked with that asked me not to mention God or not to pray for them. I have had one decide she didn't want to go to church with us, and we let her make that choice. That same child asked us to pray for her when things got rough. Even though she in no longer in my home I still get calls from her, asking what God is saying to me about her life. She continues to request that I keep her in prayer because this and such or that is happening. Even the teens I worked with in juvenile probation often ask me for prayer. Teens know fake stuff and fake people. One thing that I have never been called is a fake. They know my faith is real and that I am real. Being true to who I am as a follower of Jesus Christ is a must for me. I won't hide it for anyone.

We discussed earlier about things we are not comfortable with in our homes, and how we can take those concerns to the caseworker. The same goes for the teens that come to live with us. They need to be able to express their discomfort if our faith or anything else about our home makes them uncomfortable. This is true whether the discomfort comes from racial issues, sexual identity issues, or whatever. They should be able to be in a place where they will thrive, and as foster families we should be able to live true to who we are. Being willing to compromise and remain genuine can be a tough balancing act. Sometimes it's successful and sometimes it's not. Be encouraged, be true to who you are and what you believe. These kids are so precious and have been through so many harsh things just like so many of us. But look at us now! Never lose hope for the future of your foster teen.

"For I know the plans I have for you," says the LORD. "They are plans for good and not for disaster, to give you a future and a hope" (Jeremiah 29:11 NLT).

JUST SOME IDEAS

I have included samples of the guidelines we use for establishing ground rules for foster life. Some of you may be more lenient and some more strict about what you'll allow in your home. In our home we have had to compromise, revamp, and toss out quite a few guidelines. Flexibility is key. For some kids a certain guideline may work, while for others it might be a major problem. The guidelines might involve how friends of your teen will be handled, the "spend-the-night thing," and many other issues you may face. At the bottom of the guidelines for "keeping your family safe and peaceful" you will notice that I discuss Ouija boards and other occult activities. That is an example of an issue that is extremely important to us and we strongly enforce it. Other issues might be negotiable in our home, but that one is not. The bottom line is, do what works for your family and your child. Your absolute NO will be different from ours.

As you can see, we have the kids sign the "sharing a room and making it work" agreement because they are making an agreement with us, and with each other. When there is a violation we remind them of the agreement and the consequences. When there have been multiple infractions in a certain area, we draw up an agreement that says something like, "Because I violated curfew twice, I understand that if I violate curfew one more time the following consequences will be in effect:

_____." We ask them to sign and date this agreement, and this helps them understand that it is binding.

We invite our teens to participate in deciding on consequences that we all can agree on. That way if they violate an agreement we can say, "You came up with this consequence, not me, so I'm holding you accountable," so they can't play the blame game or get mad at us, because it was their own idea!

As I've stated over and over and over, be flexible. Things look great on paper and in our head; then real life happens and everything can get blown out of the water. If that happens, regroup.

**Guidelines to Keep the Home Peaceful and Safe
(posted on the fridge)**

- Show respect for each person, their space, property, and time.

- Participate in family meals, gatherings, and meetings.

- Participate in household chores and keeping the house clean and presentable.

- Speak to everyone in a respectful manner: calm voice, using language that is not offensive (curse words, derogatory, racial slurs etc.).

- We will be notified of guests PRIOR to them coming over and they will come over only UPON OUR APPROVAL.

- UPON OUR APPROVAL, guests of the opposite sex are to visit, ONLY in the living room or the backyard patio.

- WE MUST KNOW AND TRUST YOUR GUESTS before they are allowed to visit our home without one of us being home.

- We (your foster parents) must meet your friends prior to you hanging out with them.

- We must talk with and meet the parents before you spend the night with friends.

- We must be informed of where you are going and whom you will be with. If you decide to change your plans or are going to be late, you are to notify us.

- Please abide by the arranged curfew.

- Please keep your room reasonably clean, with a thorough cleaning weekly, i.e., sweep, mop.

- Please keep music and TV positive, with no cursing, extreme sexual content, or extreme violence unless it is on your personal audio device with headphones.

- Modest attire is expected to be worn and all personal areas are expected to be covered.

- We have a special request: do not practice the occult, Ouija boards, witchcraft, séance or anything similar in or around the home. Do not bring Ouija boards into our home.

- Please know that we care for you and love you and sometimes our answer to your request will be no. You may not understand or like our decisions, but we act in your best interest.

Kitchen Responsibilities

- The kitchen duties must be completed before the person who is responsible for them goes to bed. The rotation of duties will occur on Sundays.

- Dishes should be loaded into the dishwasher. If you use a glass, keep it and use it the rest of the day, unless it's a smoothie or something that needs a more thorough washing.

- Everyone is responsible for either washing the dishes they use, including pots, pans, etc., or putting them in the dishwasher. Wash dishes that don't go in the dishwasher.

- Wipe down counters, stove, microwave (inside and out), and refrigerator.

- Put dishes away daily.

- Sweep daily and mop up spots.

- On the day chores are rotated, everything that is listed above will be done. Please mop with steam mop.

Sharing a Room and Making It Work

- Basic guidelines: everything is about respect and consideration.

- Please understand that you are not alone in the room.

- Please respect the other person's space. Keep your clothes off the floor so that each person has access to every area of the room and it remains clean.

- Please respect the other person's property. Do not use, touch, or borrow anything that is not yours. If you would like to use something, you must ask and get approval before using.

- If the other person is resting during the day, then the person coming into the room must ask if it's okay to talk, or if the other person is resting. If the other person is resting, then you must text or whatever it takes to keep the room quiet, or you may come downstairs or sit outside to talk.

- Sleeping: If an individual is trying to sleep at night, then be considerate and turn lights out and be sure all communications are by text or computer. Please refrain from laughing, talking, and making noises. You must use your headphones and put your phone on silent. Avoid walking around and making noise. Please do all of your potentially noisy activities before the other person goes to bed.

- Respect the feelings of the other person.

- If there is a conflict, politely and respectfully bring it up to the other person. You both need to learn conflict resolution. If what you must say is not received, then please bring it to our attention. It is not snitching. We are all about having peace in our home and neither one of you should be miserable in your own room and house.

- School: During the school year, lights go out and computer and phone go off at 10:30 p.m. I can't monitor whether or not you get off the phone, but there will be no talking or use of electronics that will make noise.

- Being able to share a room and learn how to effectively communicate will take you very far. This is all a learning experience and I know you both will be successful.

- Food: please keep it downstairs. In the past I have asked that bowls and food be brought down before bed, but that was not happening. So as of now no food upstairs.

- Anything you want to add?

Signature: _____

Date: _____

REAL-LOVE STORIES

Annette, Texas

We fostered for about five years. We fostered five children, infants and toddlers, during that five-year period. Our family was classified as *Foster-To-Adopt.*

Sometimes a gift takes you by surprise.

We never intended to foster or adopt. It's not that we don't love children, and it's not even that the thought of fostering and adoption never entered our minds. Our family has always had a soft spot for little ones. We absolutely adore children and we probably would have entertained the idea of having more kids if I had been able, but the idea of fostering always seemed too risky. The thought of receiving children into our home, nurturing and caring for them, loving them like our own, and then at a moment's notice having to relinquish them back to an uncertain future was just not something we ever thought we could do. It was a terrifying thought, best left unexplored. Adoption seemed too complicated and expensive, and considering we already had three wonderful biological children, the thought of adopting even seemed a bit greedy.

The problem was, we were only thinking of how fostering and adopting would affect us—our family. One day a young military woman unexpectedly entered our lives and changed everything. I was working as a secretary in a small church when a distraught young woman came into my office in tears. She wanted to see the pastor for counsel and prayer. My heart immediately went out to her so I took her to the pastor's office. After she had an opportunity to meet with him in private, the pastor called me back into his office and asked if I would pray for her. Before I was given any information about how to pray, I was immediately driven to my knees and began sobbing out a prayer I barely remember speaking. There have been few times in my life I've prayed that way, but I will never forget the feeling of being prayed through. Both the pastor and the young woman were shocked and astounded at how accurately the prayer reflected the truth of the situation, and God put a particular continued burden on my heart to pray for that woman, even after she left that day.

Through another confounding turn of events, the same young woman ended up on the doorstep of our home a few weeks later. She had asked the pastor for a list of small groups in her area and ours was the closest location to the temporary lodging facility she was staying at on base. So there she was right before our cell group began one Wednesday evening. During that gathering we found out her story. She was four months pregnant as a result of an adulterous affair that had taken place during her deployment overseas. When her condition was discovered, her commander immediately sent her back to the states to begin discharge proceedings. When she returned home, her husband filed for divorce because of the betrayal, and that was what led her into the church that day we first met. That evening she also confessed that she did not want to keep the baby, and told us she was considering an abortion because a baby would be a constant reminder of how she ruined her marriage.

After that first night, I spent countless hours and days counseling this young woman to reconsider. Because she was already estranged from her husband and many miles away from her mother and father, my husband and I invited her to stay with our family until her discharge from military service was final. After weeks of prayer and care she decided that she wouldn't terminate her pregnancy but she also knew she did not want to raise the baby. That is when she asked my husband and me to consider adopting her unborn child. To say we were shocked would be a bit of a stretch because God had strangely begun preparing my heart for the question from the moment I first met the woman. She explained that she could never consider giving up the baby to someone she didn't know and trust, but she also never wanted to see the baby, which made a kinship adoption impossible.

My husband, my three children and I all sat down, prayed and had a serious conversation about accepting her proposal. We soon came to a unanimous decision that it was meant to be, but little did we know how our faith would be tested as a result of that decision.

We had no idea the amount of paperwork, money, and stress the verification process would take to complete all the legal requirements to adopt someone's baby. My husband had just gone into business for himself and we were barely making enough money to live on, and little-to-no money left for extras. You can imagine our anxiety when we discovered that the costs to become verified for an Identified Adoption are about $10,000!

We took the information back to God and realized the cost had not taken Him by surprise. At that point, I think it was easier for me than my husband to continue to walk in faith, because he was the sole breadwinner of our family. Knowing this, I approached him and assured him that I did not expect him to come up with all that money himself, but instead asked if we could take one step at a time and walk the journey out in faith, agreeing that if God provided the money it was His will and if He didn't, then it was never His will to begin with. That seemed to help my husband have the freedom to move forward.

Time after time over the course of the next six months God provided in crazy, scary, miraculous ways at exactly the right times. The first $1000 we needed to complete the home study was delivered in a particularly humorous way. A vendor my husband contracted with was not able to complete a job on time because of a mass power outage due to major storms in their area. As a result, they sent us a check for the inconvenience of missing the deadline. The $1000 check was sent the week before our home study was scheduled and had a simple note included that read, "Mr. Griffin, again we apologize for missing your print deadline. This could not be helped, as the storms that caused our power outage were an act of God."

The further we got into the adoption verification process the thicker the red tape became. The young woman decided to move back to Ohio to live with her mother and father and deliver the baby there, which meant interstate adoption laws would have to be observed, and a social worker in her home state would have to get involved. For six months we fervently jumped the hurdles that were presented, completed the training required, and paid the astronomical fees that were involved, all thanks to God's provision. Finally, we thought our job was done, but just weeks before the baby was born we were presented with our last challenge. In order to take the baby into our care directly from the hospital, Ohio state law required that we be certified as foster parents. We were put on a "fast track" for foster-care training and two weeks later our entire family breathed a sigh of relief. Finally, all the paperwork, legal work, and legwork were completed and we could focus on traveling to get our baby, who would soon be born through a scheduled C-section.

The balance of walking by faith, yet remaining yielded in complete surrender to God's will is a precarious business. It reminds me of a tightrope walker. He teeters on that fine line while not only defying the law of gravity but also resisting every natural inclination to wrap his arms tightly around himself to brace for a possible crash. Only by holding his arms outward, throwing all caution (and protection) to the wind can he maintain the balance needed to make it to the other side. God was teaching me that same balancing act between faith and surrender. Each week I would speak to the young woman by phone and encourage her to consider that God would equip her with everything she needed to be a good mom if she wanted to reconsider. She would often become angry with me for suggesting such a thing and adamantly reaffirm her position. Finally, she asked me to stop talking to her about keeping the baby and insisted that I give her the name we had chosen for the baby so that she could have it recorded directly on the birth certificate to avoid having to change it later.

When the time finally came for the baby to be born, it was particularly thrilling for us to make the trip up north, not just because we knew we'd be returning home with a precious bundle, but it was December and as we followed the map further and further upward, the typical brown winter terrain to which we were accustomed, being from the south, began to fade away into a crisp feathery white. The look, feel, and smell of everything fresh and new helped etch into our hearts a more intimate memory of the whole experience.

We arrived at our Ohio hotel the evening before the baby was born. The kids wanted to play in the snow, and my husband and I were experiencing major *first-time-parents-again* jitters, so the night was pretty restless. We arrived on time at the hospital the next morning and immediately were taken into the nursery. That is where we first saw, held, and showed our pent-up love to our new baby boy, Evan James. He was named after my grandfather who had passed away several years prior. Finally everything seemed to fall in place. It was finally real, not just a dream. It was at that very moment that I vividly remember feeling my spiritual arms leaving their outward balancing position and closing in quickly— along with my physical arms—to cling to the promise for which I had found myself unexpectedly longing. For six glorious hours, we lavished Evan with kisses, hugs, and caresses. He lay in my arms wide awake looking up at me with dark blue eyes and a furrowed newborn brow, as his siblings whispered secret promises into his tiny ears: future basketball games, ice cream outings, and music lessons. I wondered how I would ever be able to keep the little guy from being spoiled rotten.

Then without any fanfare or warning, the social worker entered the room and sat right across from me. With six small words, every hope, every plan for the future, and every ounce of joy was blown into oblivion, as she matter-of-factly said, "The mother has changed her mind."

Distraught and heartbroken we returned to the desolate hotel room. We had all prayed for this child and diligently prepared for him for six months. We were consumed by his presence before we ever laid eyes on him. The emptiness I felt was intensified by the fact that

I knew my husband and children were grieving in ways I would never be able to understand. We were originally told to be prepared to stay in the state for several weeks to finalize the legalities of the adoption, but with Christmas just around the corner, we had no desire to be in a foreign state with no family—and no baby. As we prepared to head home, a blizzard hit. The highways were closed for days and we missed being home for Christmas. During that time trapped in a hotel room far from our home I grieved, doubted, questioned, and cried, but I also learned to sing in the valley of Achor. I learned that His promises are not always fulfilled in the ways I perceive, and that in spite of my pain (and in the middle of it) He and His plans are still good.

Two weeks after we returned home, we received a call from our social worker. "Mrs. Griffin, I know we have never discussed this, but you are on our registered foster-care list, and I know you are prepared for an infant. I thought I'd call to let you know that we have a little boy who is five weeks old. He is just now ready to be discharged from the hospital. He has spent the first five weeks of his life withdrawing from heroine and now needs a foster home. Would you and your husband consider fostering?"

That call yielded something wonderful—a gift we never expected, and one we would have been too afraid, and too "comfortable" to accept had we not been through the difficult journey God mapped out for us to walk by faith. That call gave us our son, Josiah, and later our daughter, Faith, and three other little ones for temporary seasons along the way, in foster care. Each of those children taught us something new about God and ourselves. They all have a special calling on their lives, that we were given brief moments in time to invest in. We never knew to hope for them and never knew they needed us until that need became apparent through tragedy.

Marlena, Mississippi

I have been fostering since 2014. God gave me a strong vision to help His children. It was odd—I was dreaming about young kids of parents who had a problem with drugs. I wanted desperately to feed these children—not just food, but love, His Word, stability, and feeling safe. These are things these kids don't have.

I have had twelve children ranging in age from two to twelve. Each one of these kids came with their own set of problems—each damaged, and each of them had parents that used drugs.

At first, I worked with kids aged two to thirteen. However, I soon found that I couldn't cope with the older children. These kids had been in the system so long, and were so hurt that their parents didn't love them enough to give up drugs, that they were angry and sometimes would strike out to hurt others, including me. Now I work with kids aged two to six. I want these children to know that drug addiction is an illness and has nothing to do with them. They are loved and wanted. I give them more than just three meals a day. They have a home, love, fun, and God. I find that children that get a foundation with Christ handle adversity a little better.

I'm strictly fostering—not to say my heart doesn't go out to these kids. Many, many times I have talked to my husband about adopting one or two, but realistically, we are near retirement and these children need a family unit that has two young and able parents. They need and deserve a family that will be with them for more than the years we have left.

One thing I wish someone had told me about fostering is that there is no way to foster children without putting your heart out there. You are going to get hurt. When the time comes for these kids to move on—or better still, go home—it is bittersweet. I have grieved for my kids and yes, I call them my kids because we become a family for six months or two years. For that time, we are a family and I love each of them.

If there were one piece of advice I would give future foster parents it would be firstly, it's not about money—you don't make enough! These children come broken and without anything. You will need to supply not just love and food, but basic necessities. Grooming, clothing, school clothes, school supplies, and toys. The list is endless. I would suggest keeping a journal for each child and yourself. I would also suggest that you make a memory book and journal for each child. Some children can't write, but they can draw, so having a feelings book helps these children to understand their feelings and that it's ok to be sad, mad, or blah!

You are told that you must assume that these children come to you broken and damaged. It's hard to believe that a child with Downs Syndrome would come to you having been molested as well. These children for the most part are very happy and loving. My little girl J fell asleep on the rocking chair and without thinking I went to pick her up and place her in her bed. Wrong! This child came at me fighting and kicking and screaming. This little six-year-old kicked me so hard on my knees I lost my balance and fell into the wall, dislocating my shoulder. I cried buckets not for my pain, but for the fear I caused that little girl. It took my family hours to calm her down while I went to the ER. When I returned home, she was so upset and I was upset that I didn't think to just wake her and ask her to go to bed. I had to rock her to sleep to calm her down. Since then I always wake the children up to help them to their rooms because you don't know all they have gone through. Even two-year-olds will fight you if they've been molested.

Sadly, I don't have a feel-good story. My first foster child is still in the system going from home to home because he was bullied, and so he is a bully. My next four went home, but are back into the system. The next three siblings were split up and sent to separate homes. Their mental stability caused such conflict that it was necessary for them to be separated. Of the three I have now, two will be leaving to stay with relatives, but not with the parent that is fighting for them. This really hurts, as it is the children that suffer when grandparents and parents fight. And my little M is with me for a while so I can get her the medical help she needs. Luckily, I have the support of this one's grandparents, aunts, and uncles to help and support me while I get this sweetheart the help she needs. She is autistic and has special needs and I will fight to get whatever she needs. Sometimes these kids need you to fight for their education, so it is important that an IEP

(Individual Education Plan) is set for each of them since they move so often. Each school should know the problems that need to be addressed and assessed.

I cannot stress enough how much of a need there is for foster parents—GOOD foster parents. Even if you're in your fifties, sixties, or seventies you can be a great foster parent. Just pick the age range you are willing to work with. Get help and support from your church and from the schools. They are eager to help these children as well. You hear such horror stories about foster parents keeping kids in cages etc. How awful for these kids to go from neglect to conditions not fit for animals. The need is there. The caseworkers are so overwhelmed with kids that don't have any place to go except group homes. These children need our help. They don't have a voice so we have to be that voice for them. If you can't foster, volunteer as a CASA worker—there is one in every community. Become a voice for these little children who have no voice and no rights. My heart aches for the children we haven't rescued yet.

Steve, California

We have been foster parenting for four years, and have fostered four teenage girls. I wanted to be a foster parent. I wanted to offer these young ladies the care and love that I had given to our three bio-kids. I wanted to provide a sense of what a "normal" family is, has, and does, before launching them into adulthood.

Each of the girls came with different scars from some type of violence (family, community, parental, etc.). All had a view of a father, which I did not seem to fit, for better or worse.

My desire to help them was always there, yet my own experience as a dad was a hindrance in some instances. What I didn't consider, and was made aware of, was how different the needs of each girl were. In my mind, I was going to be some kind of hero who rescues the girls from a life of misery. That concept was blown to bits (as were my feelings) by our first foster child, a young Latina who was unable to stay with her parents but had a strong (and large) family nearby. She just wanted to graduate from high school. Period.

She was pleasant but had no (zero, zip, zilch) interest in being a part of our family. She was from a Hispanic culture, as seen in her preference for certain music, food, friends, and involvement with her family. Thus, my role was reduced to being what I did NOT want to be: a landlord.

My bio kids had sixteen years of me before they hit seventeen, so they (and I) knew what to expect for the most part going forward. But this was a brand-new world, and a foreign culture that I struggled to embrace.

I often did not understand their decisions, or their decision-making processes. I felt very inadequate as a parent for these girls. Their needs were so different from what I expected, and so deep. Realizing that you don't know everything is okay, AS LONG AS you are willing to listen and understand. This didn't always mean listening to the child, but to your spouse who probably sees things somewhat differently than you.

I am learning to listen and not jump to conclusions, or at least not to express out loud the conclusions I have jumped to.

Kasie, Tennessee

"I would foster, but…I would get too attached. I just don't think I could give them back."

This has got to be the number one reason that I hear people say for not becoming involved in #FosterCare. It's a legitimate concern—it really is. But I want to give you a few reasons why you should still consider fostering.

1) Yes. You will get attached. But, you NEED to get attached. These children need attachment. They need

healthy adults who can show them stability and unconditional love. They haven't had this. They're hurting. They need you.

2) Yes. You can give them back and you will, if that's what the court orders. You will cry and your heart will hurt, but here's the thing: fostering is not about comfort. It is all kinds of uncomfortable and sacrificial. The main goal of foster care is reunification. And this is perfectly in line with God's word, which tells us that we are to be ministers of reconciliation. Listen, this is a tangible way in which you can minister reconciliation to families who are hurting. You can be an agent of healing not only in the lives of children, but in the lives of their parents, who are also hurting.

3) Children in foster care are not always reunited with their parents. Sometimes, the situation is not healthy or safe enough for them to return. And in that case, they will be placed for adoption. If you have fostered a child through the course of their case, you will have the opportunity to become their forever family, if you choose to be.

4) If in your heart you truly believe that fostering is not in your calling, you can still adopt from foster care. Many foster care agencies license homes as "foster-

to-adopt" or "adopt only." You can work with an agency that will only place in your home children whose parental rights have been or are on their way to being terminated.

These are difficult things to talk about. We wish that no child would ever need to be in foster care. We wish that if a child did come into foster care, their parents would quickly become healthy and stable enough to be reunified with them. But the reality is that children all across America ARE in the system. They are hurting. Their parents are not yet stable and they need nurturing homes in the interim. There ARE children whose parents could not complete what the State required of them, who are now sleeping in shelters or being moved from home to home to home. They are hurting and they need nurturing forever homes.

You can make a difference. We are ALL called to care.

Grace and Love

Our daughters' doll collection reminds me of what heaven will look like.

People say children don't see color. But I believe children DO see color; and they know in their hearts that each shade of human is as beautiful as the next.

#FosterCare has exposed our family to a world of diversity on such a deeper level than we ever expected: diversity in culture, ethnicity, race, color, religion, and various social and economic backgrounds. We have been up close and personal with families of all shades, and we're better for it. Opening our home to the unfamiliar at a time when our children were still growing has helped to shape their worldview in a more positive light. It has nourished a natural inclination toward acceptance of all people. It is breaking cycles of prejudiced stereotypes, biased generalizations, and just plain wrong thinking about people different from us.

Their world will be built on tolerance, grace and love.

Jane, Texas

We fostered one sibling set of three for five months and then we adopted two girls.

I asked God what was going to happen to these girls and He showed me a momentary glimpse of them grown up. One was in prison and the other was a prostitute with three kids born to different men. That was when I said, "No! Not on my watch. Not if I have anything to do with it. They have to get a new destiny now." I asked my husband whether he thought if we adopted them we could fix them. His response was, "Part of me thinks we could, but part of me is afraid they will break our hearts." We realized that we couldn't let fear keep us from what God was calling us to do, enabling us to do, and putting us in the position to do. We can raise them and train them to be healthy citizens and they won't get that in the foster system—they need parents.

We decided to adopt the girls. When we told the girls we asked CPS (Childhood Protective Services) if we could adopt them and that CPS had said yes, we asked the girls if they would like for this to be their forever family. Overnight, over half of J's behavior problems went away! She was seven. Half of her behavior problems were steeped in insecurity. The other behavioral problems were typical kid stuff: poor training, a little bit of inborn genetics stuff. But half of it was just insecurity, and that proved it. Right then and there we knew that we would never go back to being foster parents again because we really feel like we can't be the kind of parents we're supposed to be within the confines or restraints of the foster system. We had a placement before the girls. It was a sibling set of three and they reunited with their dad, and that was a resounding success in terms of the mentoring we were able to provide for the dad during his journey to get the custody of his kids back. We were able to reunify those kids and thought, "Hey, we're pretty good foster parents; let's do this again!" Then we got the girls and we were like, "Whoa! They don't train you for this!" There is no way they could write a book for all the different scenarios that you will encounter.

Darlene, Nevada

We have been fostering for ten years and have had twenty-two kids come through our home. We have adopted three and we are currently fostering two. I would say the best advice would be to understand that no two kids are alike, and all social workers are different. When I say different I mean that each social worker has his or her own way of dealing with the kids on their caseloads.

Your best support systems are other foster parents or families. I enjoy seeing the lives of the kids change and being a lifeline for the family.

Christine, Mississippi/Germany

We fostered one child for ten days.

My maternal grandfather deserted his family during the depression and as a result, my mother and her siblings went into foster care. At the time, many people did foster care as a way to make money, and treated the children very cruelly. This was the situation with my mother and her first two foster homes. In the third foster home, she found a safe, loving haven and a woman who treated her like her own child. My husband and I talked about my mom's experience a lot and while we were stationed overseas in Germany we decided to become foster parents ourselves with the idea that we would provide a loving safe-haven to children in need. We wanted to help them through tough times. We went through the training, background investigation, etc., and about three months later received a call from a social worker. They were removing an eleven-year-old girl from her family and needed emergency care. The little girl came from a Nigerian family and the father's discipline methods were quite different from what the US military found acceptable. Our daughter had bunk beds in her room and we hoped the little girl would enjoy the company of someone close in age. We were very optimistic that we could help, as many people are when they go into foster parenting. The first night went better than we hoped even though our foster daughter was visibly uncomfortable with the fact that we were a white family and she was Nigerian, her skin a beautiful ebony color. The next day was Sunday, and we all went off to church together, which went well. When we got home, our foster daughter told us she was going to take a shower, which was fine, except that she locked herself purposely in our only bathroom for the next hour, which created some issues. When she finally came out, she didn't recognize that this had been a problem even though we explained the only toilet in the house was in that bathroom and both of our kids had to go to a neighbor's to use their bathroom. That night, our daughter woke up to our foster daughter going through her memory box and taking a few things out, which she stashed in her suitcase. She told me about it the next morning and when I asked our foster daughter about it she denied taking anything. When we opened her suitcase she said, "I don't know how they got there." As the days went on, we noticed food and snacks missing, which I found when I looked in her luggage. Even though

I told her she could eat whatever she wanted whenever she wanted, she would still take and hide food. Then we noticed our dog behaving strangely around her, as if he were scared. She said dogs didn't belong in a house—it was just wrong. We never saw her mistreat the dog but he was always on edge around her. After ten days, the social worker said that she would be returned to her family two nights later. I washed and packed her clothes and talked to her about being safe, about manners and respecting her parents, and told her we would pray for them to get along better. When the social worker came to pick her up, she just looked at us, turned around and left. Thankfully in a military community there isn't a lot of need for foster care and she was our only foster child during the time we were in Germany.

Priscilla, Nevada

I was the bio-child of foster parents. For most of the time as a child I wasn't a fan of foster care. It was very hard for me to share my parents since I was the youngest and felt like I was getting replaced and set aside. I was homeschooled until my parents decided to do foster care. That what's really angered me the most: that they didn't have time to teach me anymore because of foster care, and I hated public school. Now I'm grateful for that but at the time I wasn't. I felt like foster care was forced upon me and I wanted nothing to do with it. It wasn't until I got older—about the time I began driving—that I didn't mind it so much. I was no longer waiting to be picked up because a baby was sleeping or had a doctor's appointment, and I was at the age where I began to realize that I could have a positive impact on the foster kid's life, and I wanted that. I no longer wanted to be a bad memory for them.

Mimi, California

I have fostered for over twenty years. I have fostered 117 children of all ages. I am a specialist for baby care but cared extensively for all ages.

My advice is this: kids come into care traumatized by the removal from their home. They are fragile and upset and need to be treated gently. That being said, they also figure out quickly that they can manipulate and control an environment, so it is important to set standards, establish routines, and be clear about expectations, so that the kids can feel security and understand parameters.

Carol, California

I have been a foster parent for eighteen and a half years. I have fostered fifty-one children. Flexibility is key. Any time you think things are going to go a certain way, don't trust it. Situations and circumstances are always subject to change. Learn to accept this and be able to alter your path at any time. Being a foster parent is such a rewarding experience. I am constantly told what a great thing I do, but in reality, every child I care for teaches me something and adds richness to my life.

Angele, Nevada

I always say being a foster parent was one of the BEST and the most CHALLENGING things I've ever done.

The first and most surprising lesson I learned as a foster mom was about forgiveness. WHAT? This was supposed to be about the KIDS, not ME, right? It happened when I learned what our first foster daughter's parents had done to her. I was appalled and angry. She was seven years old and had suffered neglect and emotional and physical abuse. I could see the scars on her body. I could sense them in her spirit. When the time came for me to take her to a supervised visit with her parents I felt like they didn't deserve to see her. I certainly didn't want to meet them! I had a lot of emotions and judgments flying around inside.

Although I didn't say anything out loud about how I felt I knew instantly that my negative thoughts would be detrimental to the situation. I realized I had stepped into a world in which I would have influence, not only on children, but on biological families, social workers, judges, advocates, and so many others. My responses to parents could make a way for healing and hope, or could be one more roadblock of judgment and disdain. The kids would subconsciously know how I felt and it would make a difference in how they coped with the situation themselves.

I made a decision to step out in forgiveness and ask God for help to do so. It didn't mean I approved of the horrible abuse. It didn't mean I trivialized what our girl had gone through. It did not mean there was an instant transformation in how I felt. It DID mean I was able to work with the team to ultimately do the very best thing for this little girl. Sometimes that means going home (which most kids want to do), sometimes it means family placement, and sometimes it means adoption. As I kept my heart open to walk in forgiveness and love, progress was made all around. Ultimately, the parents of this precious girl were able to let go of her and she was placed with her grandparents. It was a very good place for her.

Willingness to forgive and leave the outcome to God afforded me many opportunities to mentor biological moms. That was something I couldn't imagine doing when I was in training. It ultimately became one of the most rewarding parts of my time as a foster parent.

I was naïve to think foster parenting wouldn't put me through changes. If you are called to this amazing world of helping children in their darkest hours you WILL learn, change, and grow. It is a life-changing ride and I am thankful for it.

Barbara, California

Myth versus Fact: I can't be a resource/foster parent because I would get too attached.

It's true, you WILL get attached. It's true, it IS hard to see them leave. These children need you to fall in love with them, to demonstrate unconditional love and support, as well as to provide consistency and stability. All foster/resource parents have developed their own techniques to come through each fostering experience with their hearts whole. Understanding and believing in your role as this child's advocate and support system AND as their cheerleader in the reunification process helps tremendously when it is time to say goodbye. And while saying goodbye is never easy, it is important to keep in mind that this child had to say goodbye to their family when they were placed with you, and they survived! Be inspired by their strength and you will find your own, right when you need it.

I wrote the following in my prayer journal on a day when I was frustrated listening to people complain about the children they were fostering in their home:

Love the children like they're your own, even though you are answerable to others.

Take them to visits. Be kind to bio families. Then go home and love the child some more.

Talk to the social worker/Seneca worker/lawyer/therapist/doctor/dentist when they call and ask for the same info over and over again. Then go home and love the child some more.

Make the appointments you are directed to make, even if you disagree or it doesn't work with your schedule. Then go home and love the child some more.

These situations are part of foster care and if you fight the system, wallow in the frustration, and sink into cynicism, then you WILL hate every moment and spend valuable time fighting, wallowing, and sinking when you could be lifting the child up and away from those very same emotions.

Fix what you can, accept what you can't, then go home and—oh, guess what—love the child some more.

ABOUT LESIA

Lesia is the mother of three adult children, a Gigi (grandma), and shares life with her amazing husband of thirty-six years. She is a foster parent, life coach, parent coach for parents of troubled teens, and mentor to at-risk youth.

Her love for the kids no one wants to deal with has earned her such titles as "The Teen Whisperer," and "Crazy." To Lesia, these are badges of love.

She regularly shares her keen insights and experiences with parents of at-risk youth and those looking to strengthen family relationships. Lesia is also an international motivational speaker, bringing hope and real answers for real life.

For more information or to contact Lesia to speak at your event, visit her website Lesiaknudsen.com or email her at Lesia@lesiaknudsen.com.

Made in the USA
San Bernardino, CA
04 February 2018